What People are Sc

I was deeply moved as I read Gabriella s story. I admire her honesty and courage and her willingness to share part of her life in hopes of helping others to face their pain. She writes, "you may wonder why I have shared my story so late in life"? Yet what is important is that she did share the story. I encourage you to read carefully each word and allow the story to give you courage, and bring healing to you. In the end we all need to take off our masks and live authentic lives.

– Pastor Thomas

There comes a moment in everyone's life, if they are lucky enough to be aware of it, when someone else's words of wisdom inspire real and profound change. Reading Nicole's poignant, and beautifully written journey of acceptance was that moment for me. This came at just the right moment in my life, I needed this verbal hug more than I realized and I am certainly a better version of myself because of it.

– Bridie O'Hagan – Business Executive

I enjoyed Wanda's poems. Her simplistic writing style was refreshing! At the same time the reader can feel the soulful energy of what she was trying to portray in the poems. The understanding of the process of what happens when we die has been questioned from the beginning of time. In her poems, Wanda portrays what she feels about the end of life process.

– Kathy S

Chrisanthi's story of strength and determination to overcome a tragic accident along with her raw emotion was felt through every word in this very emotional story. Her recall of sights and sounds that she experienced as she lay helpless and horribly injured after her fall made me feel as though I was with her. She writes passionately and eloquently in this story of hope and courage. Kudos Chrisanthi! You are brave beyond words!

– Jennifer Cairo, author

The divine unfolds in a beautifully written, intensely vulnerable, and sacred telling of a systematic and deeply dark journey through loss, depression, and anxiety culminating in a spiritual awakening dredged in enlightenment, new life, and an overwhelmingly joyful experience of God's light.

Jessica's chapter is a must-read for all who are just beginning to sense the existence of divine enlightenment, those working to unpack the multitude of layers that hide their true selves, those on the brink of sensing a need to release deep-rooted, negative energy hindered by darkness in their past that is both externally derived and self-imposed, as well as for those who have already gotten there.

– Veruchka Roque
Executive Consultant, MBA, MS

Jenny does a wonderful job at conveying how devastating life events can reveal to us the ways in which we are both woven into and creators of our destiny. Her story offers warmth regarding the value of family, and reminds me that where you come from is equally as important as where you are going. Her journey shows that recognizing ancestral origins and the repeated patterns presented within your family tree are necessary to heal the future generations within your family, but also yourself. This is a wonderful read about how the right perspectives can foster spiritual growth. Her experiences reveal the power of being able to view your life events, both positive and negative, as a powerful tool for your transformation; if you chose to use them as such. Jenny has learned in her own life, she has taught others as well.

– Casey Tallant

I am impressed by the rigorous honesty Ms. Perdue demonstrates on her journey. She is brave and plunges deeply into the "belly of the beast." Deborah is a living sage—an earthling willing to examine herself and soar freely—achieving that sublime balance between the literal and the ethereal.

– Lee Inkmann, M.A. Educational Studies

Awakening the Consciousness of Humanity

When Your Eyes Open
to See the Truth

A COLLECTION OF PERSPECTIVES

Nicole Walker, Jessica Mariah,
Jenny Macomber, Wanda Snyder,
Gabriella De Cicco, Chrisanthi Voukatidis
Deborah Perdue, Gloria Coppola

Authors:
Nicole Walker
Jessica Mariah
Deborah Perdue
Jenny Macomber
Wanda Snyder
Gabriella De Cicco
Chrisanthi Voukatidis
Gloria Coppola

Published by:
Powerful Potential & Purpose Publishing
Website: www.PPP-publishing.com
Email: gloria@gloriacoppola.com

Design by Deborah Perdue, Illumination Graphics
Artwork courtesy of DepositPhotos.com and Shutterstock.com

ISBN: Paperback 978-1-7361839-2-2
ISBN: Ebook 978-1-7361839-3-9

Contents

"Consciousness blooms
with the
expansion of the heart."

— Lindsay Godfree

"No one is more enlightened than another ~ They are just more comfortable in their own light,"
Gloria Coppola

OPENING INSIGHTS

*L*ies! Every day in every way we live in lies. You heard me! Let the truth be revealed as you live deeper in your heart and your perspective will shift.

As humanity is moving into a time where many are seeking the real truth, the witness to our soul journey and how much we have literally hidden behind our own mask; don't you think 2020 was a à propos time for us to lift the veil of illusion? What is truly the real pandemic in our own life?

When we are ready to remove the mask, the one created through many indoctrinations, limitations and misinformation, creating a lack of worthiness, imagine what you might discover. We are being guided by a sacred source to reveal our soul's truth. It takes courage and we may not be willing to go deeper. You see, we have stages which allow us to discover and become more comfortable with the truth of our purpose. You may manifest differently, removing lower vibrations and friendships in your life. When you are called to serve, life will shift.

Perhaps a latent gift where you can help others is tugging at you to share. Imagine if you claimed it? Would your insights and perspective shift? Has deception always been around you? Would love and relationships look differently? Would you realize you were more self-centered, and ego driven than you ever imagined? Whoa–that's a tough one!

Would you be willing to shed the mask of shame and guilt to heal yourself and others? Would you release judgements you may have owned for decades to free yourself and accept who you are?

Each author's story has a piece of their own awakening, and together they bring light, revelations and inspiration for the reader to gain more insights.

What if the truth, a horrible truth, opened your eyes to global lies? How would you receive this information? Denial at first? Fear and disbelief? Would you choose to live more authentically and heal your own deep emotional pain? Perhaps these insights are for us to release the history of abuse by stepping into our voice for those who are meek. I believe you would find greater purpose and create a ripple effect of healing out to the universe.

Awakening happens on many levels and at different times which align with our true purpose. Awareness is the awakening of the soul into a higher consciousness. Raising our frequency will stretch our comfort zone, sometimes making us mad or confused as it prepares us to make choices of One's own truth.

We are here to awaken from illusion, perhaps become a way shower. Your core essence will nudge you and unwrap you to tap into your divinity and serve from a higher platform as an emissary with a ministry to help others.

All you have to do is tune out the lies, the paradigms you believed that have not served you. Easy? Probably not for most, but when you are ready to reconnect with the soul of nature, you will be driven and unstoppable. You will notice synchronicities, have vivid dreams or insights as the cosmic consciousness aligns you with the Christ Consciousness.

You will identify sources of pain and enter the shadow side to heal. It may seem isolated at first as the healing occurs. You may not have support or understanding from others around you, however, remember changing the frequency of your thought alters the energy while you apply the element of self-love. Alchemy will create a desired result as you forgive yourself and the illusion of separation to awaken to your truth.

These stories will present to you how the victim plays out, how the absence of self-love, blame or responsibility can literally create further discord and separation. The greater revelation will unravel and your true purpose, not a job or career, will be received in the true conscious journey you embark upon with our authors. This is the passage humankind can co-create to live in higher wisdom. Allow yourself to enter the center of your heart and prepare as your healing begins here. Recognize the illusions, the martyr role perhaps you played and make a decision to step into your soul expression and the truth of your existence.

It is our desire to encourage you to understand yourself at the level you are stepping into now. We do not compare who is the greater developed because that is simply the ego creating another illusion. A child can have greater wisdom and innocence to recognize the truth than a 50-year-old highly education person, who accepted everything they were taught and neglected their soul essence.

As Rumi stated, "Doing as others told me I was blind. Coming when others called me, I was lost. Then I left everyone, myself as well. Then I found everyone, myself as well."

"To be nobody, but yourself in a world which is doing its best day and night to make you like everybody else, means to fight the hardest battle which any human being can fight and never stop fighting."

ee cummings

Let it begin.

"Nothing is random, nor will
anything ever be, whether a long
string of perfectly blue days that
begin and end in golden dimness,
the most seemingly chaotic
political acts, the rise of a great
city, the crystalline structure of a
gem that has never seen the light,
the distributions of fortune, what
time the milkman gets up, the
position of the electron, or the
occurrence of one astonishing
frigid winter after another."

— Mark Helprin

$\mathcal{N}$icole Walker

This is Nicole Walker's first published story. She has what she calls "an interesting and diverse life" with experiences that she wants to write more about.

A graduate from the American Musical and Dramatic Academy, she studied voice for over 10 years, and held leads in regional theatre including Carousel and My Fair Lady.

Nicole has worked in the fragrance manufacturing industry for over 20 years and in between worked with developmentally disabled, travelled the world and received her health coach certificate from the Integrative Institute of Nutrition.

Happily married for 25 years, Nicole has a wonderful 18-year-old son and a pet bird (caique parrot) that acts like she rules the roost. She feels blessed.

Nicole can be contacted at nicolewalkerwellness@gmail.com

Dedication

My story is dedicated to My husband George and son Rex. My rocks!

Nothing is Random

"*Y*ou're safe my love, you're safe. God loves you so much. You have been his faithful servant," I whispered to Richard as he lay dying. I've become a little too familiar with death – having already experienced my dad's and coworker's deaths within a year's time - and here I've willingly volunteered with another. *Ah! What's wrong with me? Why didn't I just take a vacation instead – alone – in silence? "I need a mental break, God. Why am I doing this AGAIN? Why ??!!!"*

Let me step back a few years; it seemed like forever watching the tremors in my dad's body take over as he slowly lost physical and mental ability. On my evening visits, he'd lay immobilized in bed, having deep meaningful conversations with me, almost like we were old friends catching up after decades apart. His mathematician's mind rambling on about Einstein and relativity, spurting out equations he discovered as a kid, laughing like he finally understood the calculations of things . . . and all he spoke were mumbled sounds. He was dying from Parkinson's, and now the most intelligent man I ever knew was speaking in a language I did not understand. I never thought I was as astute or insightful as my dad, and now I was losing the ability to ever gain any of his wisdom. My fault.

Why didn't I take the time to ask about his life growing up? Ask about his dogs. His parents. His childhood. How he got so smart. What books he read. I wasted a lot of my youth on nonsense. Was I pretty? Would I be noticed? Why was I the fat one? My entire trajectory growing up was "I just wanted to be loved unconditionally, like I imagined Cinderella felt as Prince Charming whisked her away." Did I imagine myself some forgotten princess? Was it because I was the runt in the family yearning to be noticed and loved? Is food my companion to fill the void of loneliness?

On the day he died, I asked to be alone with him. 48 years of emotions flooded through me. I stuttered, "Dad?". I knew whatever I said, I would not get a reply.

This was our final tête-à-tête. *"You're dying",* like he hadn't already figure it out. I knew he and mom didn't talk about him was dying, mentioning death was forbidden in our home. Here I was, with the courage of a 5-year-old, narrating what was happening to him. Softly, I stuttered more, "All I ever wanted to know was . . . was . . . was I ever your princess?" I felt stupid. My dad on the doorstep of death, embarking on the next journey, and I'm thinking about me. Maybe he had questions too, like; Is this the correct exit? Do I have everything I need? Shit, did that bill get paid. "I'm sorry", as if trying to make up for my childish question, acting adult (in my mind), thanking him for everything. "Oh, and Dad," whispering in his ear while kissing the 5 o'clock shadow on his cheek, letting it gently scratch my face. "You call the shots on who you want around when you finally pass. Do you want to be alone, or with mom, or us? You design how you want it. Use your energy to draw it when it's time." I brushed the roughness of his cheek once more, kissing stubble that knew not to stop growing as he died, and I quietly left.

A few hours later, I received a call to return, "This was 'it', get here fast, any second now." I inhaled deeply, resolving not to panic, instead mentally preparing myself I may miss 'that' moment, reassuring the longing of my inner child this was how it was supposed to be, as long as my mom was there. Forty minutes later, I was re-familiarized with the walls which cradled imminent heartache and entered; he hadn't died yet. In seconds, my mom scuffled everyone out to the narrow hall (my sister, brother, herself) offering me a few extra moments. I knew immediately . . . "Dad? Did you wait for me?" In his quiet face I saw peace, new knowledge and a universe of love for his little girl. I faintly blurted out, "You WAITED for me! You wanted me here too! I am your princess," tears streaming down my cheeks. They told him I was coming, and he waited. He could have left; he had every right to do so. This was his end-of-life story, yet he stayed until we were all there, including me. Had he really heard me earlier? Was he telling me something? Did he wait to make sure I knew I was his princess, staying to include me, instead of feeling left out? In his stillness he spoke like a prince, then was off. It was beautiful, the four of us crowding around him like we were cooing over a newborn, as he *birthed into a new journey.* Not a journey of physical presence, but spirit. Our cooing was really tears of grief as we let go. My hand touching his fading warmth, saying "goodbye, I love you" one last time, like a young girl chasing a train, hoping her voice would carry over the release of steam as it embarked. I think I felt his soul lift to heaven right then. At one point I looked up to the ceiling see if he was hovering above us, to see more than just the crowns of our heads. I smiled lovingly at the ceiling. Then my eyes darted back to his physical body, and I was grounded in his stillness. His suffering was over. I imagined he was like a butterfly emerging from the cocoon, about to take flight with colored wings that spoke a story. Is death life's transformation? The soul emerging from a chrysalis, finally fully developed. Only he and God knew all the details to his life on earth now. I believe they had curated his journey long ago before he was born and he followed it, to the decimal. Maybe this was his reward for following it, a peaceful death surrounded by loved ones. Maybe this wasn't random, maybe it was as calculated as an algebraic equation. It was so intimate, so graceful, structurally planned out by a higher power. My dad, the scholar, shared his most valuable knowledge that evening; We are only lent to one another. We come from God and return to God. Nothing in life is random, is it God?

I just had this beautiful life experience watching my dad die, but the grief was bigger. I would have these sudden moments, where sometimes I felt my spirit was screaming in outer space unheard. Other times I would stand in the middle of a highway with everything whirling by me. It was unpredictable.

Overeating and drinking became good companions, covering up quite a bit. Driving and meditating didn't calm me. Sometimes I'd grab a crystal off the windowsill to feel the energy. I wasn't feeling anything but a hard rock in my palm. Had I become a nobody because I wasn't feeling anything? I believed I had a destiny greater than this. I knew I was meant to help others, or at least I wanted to help others, I needed to snap out of it. I decided to work on shifting my perceptions, maybe follow The Secret, test the Laws of the Universe to see if it really worked and prayed a lot "dear God, I need you…" My thoughts would trail off into the abyss. If there really was a God, he/she/they knew all about my struggles. I'm sure they heard the throbbing echo of my grief even when I didn't speak. But nothing in my life was changing. My prayers became emphatic; "Ok God, this isn't working for me anymore. I mean like what the deal here?!". Now I'm mad, which felt good! "All of this is changing" I'd chant enraged, demanding God to make it better. "You gotta give me something more than this GOD! I'M OWED" And that's just what he did, gave me more; my prayers answered. Be careful what you wish for . . . Eleven months later, my co-worker was killed. He was wonderfully sarcastic, charismatic, shamanistic and an alcoholic. He was my friend who I admired. His death was startling, yet deep down I knew it was inevitable. Just wish it didn't happen after we had spent the last few days of his life together. WHY DID THIS HAVE TO HAPPEN? This wasn't random, was it God? If you knew this was going to be his last few days, why was he with me and not his family? What was the POINT of this GOD?

I felt a soulful change in him before we went travelling across Europe together; he was peaceful. How'd he do it? I wanted to know more. Find out *His Secret*, and was it something that would work for me too. I knew travelling through England and Germany alone was going to give me plenty of opportunity to ask him. I pictured us having long heartfelt discussions, like girl-friends sharing giggles and secrets, but I didn't ask him much of anything. I was afraid it might embarrass him. Really, I didn't want to embarrass myself. Why was I so afraid to have intimate conversations when there was so much healing that could be done?

It seemed any time I'd start personal conversations, I'd hear this voice scolding me. "Don't ask such questions, it's none of your business! You wouldn't understand. Nosy". "I'm not! I care! I love people" my 5-year-old self-yelling back, feeling so misunderstood. Did I only have 'meaningful' conversations because my sly ego wanted to hear stories of insecurities to feel superior? Or was I psychically picking up on what people really thought when conversing with me? It became easier not to talk at all.

I was heartbroken when I heard about his death and wanted to apologize to his family and give back that time. But there are no give backs with death. Why did we even go? Damn it! Oh, I know why. I wanted to have an excuse to be away from the everyday. This was my idea . . . had I'd known! Life is just so precious. He showed me.

Fast forward two years and everything I ever thought was about to change. "Nicole, I love you, you are so beautiful and so wonderful." "Richard darling, you're gay. Don't you remember?" My heart knew he needed someone, but did I know that "someone" would end up being me? Ha! Cinderella to the rescue!

Growing up, I was always acting; playing the timid girl saved from the perils of the world by the handsome prince, escaping loneliness and fear of being called "fat." I loved feeling loved. I wanted more of it! I wanted to go to acting school so I could play like this every day! Acting school was life changing, it helped me grow up. I unmasked new realms of emotions which were wonderfully intense, that is when I wasn't talking with my therapist. Playing roles revealed the psyche; emoting beyond the superficial, channeling the very real; inter-weaving complexities of the involuntary attitudes that shape and carve the ego. Discovering abstract perspectives juxtaposed to safety of my own. I started to see *into* people and quietly study their souls. Their presence totally mesmerized me, while figuring out the importance of their tiniest movements, a scratch, a twitch. Did they mean to do that, or was it reassurance of their existence? Are they confident or introverted? Do they understand what drives them? Was this helping my acting or really helping me? I'd visualize opening, my sixth chakra, the third eye, awakening from my human slumber, teaching me a new skill, *empathy*. This did not feel random, it felt purposeful.

Nothing's ever typical with me. Back then, I always felt different from my peers. I'd reassure myself 'it was ok' carving my path, letting time shape me like an old soul with intricate knowledge. Acting was giving me new depth. An understanding for life I hadn't grasped and a connection to past lives which ran parallel in my present. I didn't want to be the waiflike ingénue anymore, needing protection, (f'k that) I wanted roles of substance, of human confusion, of what life really was about! I felt I finally was growing up! It was time to let go of my inner child! I just hoped she understood and didn't feel abandoned.

I prayed the Universe would show me more. This new spirituality 'thing' was indescribable. "Please God, show me more". Enter Richard, my conduit to the more. I knew he wasn't random; I knew he was divinely placed!

It was glorious, my weekly voice lessons. Richard instructed me as we fine-tuned my vocal cords. I worked myself like a prima donna, so I could achieve high soprano pitches touching upon the stars of heaven. I would visualize energy releasing from my body, spinning upwards like golden light, a clear path reverberating to God . . . the precise metronome-like timing of Richard's hands gliding up and down piano keys, guided my pitches. So pure, this was the intimacy I had longed for. A relationship where words were not needed. Our understanding of each other's creativity; immersing ourselves, cloaked by veils of purples, blues, reds, and yellows as dusk settled in. There was so much more to life and art than I knew. Suddenly I had this 'relationship'! It felt authentic, and I wasn't questioning if I had secret motives. It was *my voice only* I heard! I was singing! And asking questions too!

Sometimes I'd ask him to treat me to his newest compositions. The pianist extraordinaire magically connecting harmonies as profound as the vocal scales we practiced. Playing melodies which resonated from deep within; were they chords that echoed for love? How did he know to plunk out these notes? Was it random? Or was he guided by the divine? All of this carried me out of the mundane, putting me into a melodic trance drawing me closer to my spirituality. It so was enlightening.

Seven years later, he abruptly told me he was passing me on to another teacher. Surprised, I felt rejected, though our time together became chore-like. I hadn't really been saying much anymore. The familiar voice was back and scolding me to be quiet. Was he jealous I had gotten married? I felt a sense of loyalty to him. Besides, a few years back, he asked me to be his health proxy. Was this just a kind nod to our friendship, or did he really trust me? He had no family or relatives. He was aging like a piano losing its tune. Did he think he was going to die alone?

Honestly, I was honored at the time someone knowingly entrusted **ME** with their life. Now no one to compete with when speaking. No voices putting me down. Finally, I was to be heard; I was his chosen co-conductor. I thought nothing of it as I harmoniously agreed to be his power of attorney. Did I really understand what I was getting into? *NAH*! I romanticized the situation;

I was helping to save his soul. Maybe our relationship was blossoming into more after all these years, even though I had a child. I always felt Richard and I were more than teacher and student; we were a duet of a higher existence. And now I'm frenziedly signing legal documents that hold me solely responsible for his life? What am I really doing with myself here? I signed on to be a knight in shining armor?!

My life was like a boulder catching speed rolling downhill as I stood in its path, shuffling him around to nursing homes, chasing after his affairs, learning medical terms, traveling for work, taking care of my family, etcetera . . . **What a process.** No wonder I was exhausted. I willingly accepted to do this too! What was wrong with me? During this entire time, I had over-whelming guilt for spending the last two weeks with someone right before he was killed. This was like a huge joke and I was the punch line. Really, how would I manage all of this, let alone grieve another death... Screw You God!

What exactly was God calling me to do? Had God been polishing me like a diamond? Cutting facets of compassion in me? Was I to be the conductor in the maestro's final composition? Was God using me in a greater way than I had realized all this time - just not how I had pictured (me in a beautiful pink gown sashaying to the needy, while fixing my lipstick).

These deaths were my experiences too. I was cast a crucial role in each one. None of this was random, it was composed. Then, I realized the immense love and joy I experienced with my dad and friend; I wanted Richard to know this too. My heart raced. Was this what I was being asked to do? Share in the gift of love and joy so generously shared with me and made me feel important, like I imagined a princess would feel? WAIT! You mean I WAS a princess all along surrounded by endless love?! How could I have missed this?! I wasted so much time on what I fantasized; I wasn't getting versus nurturing everything I did have! The realization was tremendous. It all came into focus. Even as tears flooded my eyes, the years of confusion cleared. I had experienced ALL OF THIS so I could understand Richard, feel the depth of empathy God wanted him to have. I didn't want him to die alone. I wanted to be present with him and LET HIM KNOW LOVE.

Watching him deteriorate was like watching members of an orchestra, one by one, pack up their instruments and leave the music pit. It was just a matter of time, maybe moments, of shallow breaths that he dies. I stroked his arm gently repeating *"You're safe my love, you're safe. God loves you so much. You have been his faithful servant."* I heard a crack in my voice. He had been sleeping for days as if cast under a spell. Had I become the evil witch by controlling his last few years? I liked that he was sleeping. Maybe this way when God came to get him, he'd be less afraid... maybe he'd think it was a dream. Many visits I'd watch his pensive eyes and wonder what he was thinking. I'd ask, but he never answered until once. He grabbed my hand, squeezed it tightly and said it worried him God would turn him away. He cried hard; *was this 85 years of emotion coming out?* My heart melted, all I wanted to do was hold him like a son. He was God's gift to me, my opportunity to learn how to give love unconditionally. He humbled and grounded me, making my inner princess feel needed. "Oh, Richard, you are God's precious child. He adores you. You have done *everything* exactly the way God wanted. He's so proud of you. He's going to welcome you with arms wide open, embrace you when it's time. Until then I get you." I listened to his sounds as he cried. They pulled me back into the melodic trances that once drew me so close to my spirituality. It was like he was composing his last piece, and it was his most beautiful.

I felt peaceful inside, leaning over to kiss his cheek. I told him how much I was going to miss him and whispered for him not to wait any longer. "*Go when you need to. If you want me there, show me, if you don't, I understand.*" Then I asked him to please escort me to heaven when it's my turn (years from now). Kissed him again and hummed, "*I love you, Richard. Thank you for all of this*". I walked out into the chilly afternoon. Dusk was settling in, the sky beautiful, and I felt a soothing joy overcome me. I knew by the familiar veils of purples, blues, reds, yellows coloring the sky, this could be the day. Wondering if heaven's golden rays would envelop him, create a halo around him, guide him home. Maybe God had come in quietly that day and waited. All was well. It was better than well; it was divine guidance. Later, when I was home telling my family the latest, my cell rang. It was the nursing home, "Nicole, Richard died." I quietly gasped. A multitude of emotions ran through me at once, sorrow, happiness, relief, pride in Richard. I whispered, "We did it God, thank you."

I never really put the pieces of our relationship together before, never thought of the parallels between us. Richard and I both wanted acceptance, to feel safe, be authentic . . . loved. When we first met, he willingly accepted me, embraced my needs and now I willingly embraced his needs, for better and for worse, out of love.

Sometimes I think it's not the things that happen to us which matter, as much as our willingness to be involved. It might seem easier to be a deer in the head-lights, watching the moments pass, but that's not living fully. I used to have a dialogue with God asking why life was happening to others and not me. And all God wanted to do was to wake me up. Odd how he taught me about life through death. God, in all his wisdom, had intertwined souls in a way only I could understand, even when I didn't want to, awakening me to be fully present. Awakening my consciousness to be involved and learn how to give love.

I don't mean the concept of love because we don't know what tomorrow brings or love where you make an apple pie for your grumpy husband. Yeah, it's all that, but *to love people, even those you don't know, in all their being, simply for their existence.* Could it be the people we see as we live day to day need to feel compassion too? We are all going through life lessons. Maybe a smile lets them know they're ok, accepted for who they are at that moment and helps them on their journey in ways we aren't to know. Do they remind you of you, do you need to show yourself compassion too? No one is born thinking, "I want to be a lost soul!" We are born out of love from God... we are born because GOD wanted us to be here. He picked us. He picked

YOU . . . for a gazillion reasons. No one could ever take your place. If it wasn't you, then it just wouldn't be. *Nothing is random with God. He put us here on purpose and with purpose.*

These were some of the hardest and most loving times. I wouldn't trade them. I know there's more to come, no one gets a free pass. *Because God doesn't do things randomly.* I know he guides me; it gives me peace and reassurance. I pray he continues to awaken me, and for me to follow his signs! I know he loves me. I know he loves you. Peace.

*"Do not go gentle
into that good night.*

*Rage, rage against
the dying of the light."*

— Dylan Thomas

Jessica Mariah

has longed to learn who she is and her purpose in this life, as long as she could remember. She always knew she had a special mission here on Earth. She loves so deeply but has struggled to love herself all her life. Jessica has trudged through life and fought for a life filled with love.

At age 38, she met the love her life. Nearly four years later, at almost 42 years of age, Jessica gave birth to a beautiful baby girl. This family she created, which includes her 13-year-old stepdaughter, was God's biggest gift to her.

Jessica has walked herself through the dark and found her light and God within, and she is determined to guide humanity to walk through their darkness, heal their pain and deepest wounds. Jessica longs for people to connect with their true divine selves and unite with their true God within.

Jessica's journey has led her to embrace all of who she is, her most magical gifts, and her service to God. She is an Energy Healing Facilitator, Intuitive Freedom Guide, Anxiety Coach, Breakthrough Coach, Quantum Inner Child Healing Specialist, Inspirational Speaker, and most recently has embraced her path as a Priestess.

Email: jessica@jessicamariah.com
Website: https://jessicamariah.com/

Dedication

I dedicate this to my daughter, Jade!

"Jade, I fight every day to clear myself of all turmoil and trauma for you! I know how trauma works, it's generational, and I do not want you ever to inherit any of my traumas or issues. You may have your trials and tribulations in life, but may they be YOURS, and not MINE!

Life comes with many challenges, but I want you to power through them and be the fierce and loving warrior you are, with God in your heart guiding your way! May you never give up, keep fighting and be the light in this world and the Heaven on Earth I am determined to create for you! I love you so much, my Jadie Girl!"

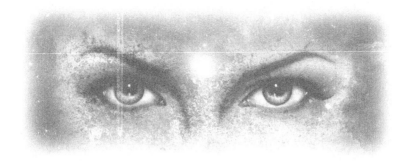

2020 Shocked Me Out of My Sleep . . .

*M*y world was shattered. It felt like the sky was falling; the Earth was crumbling beneath my feet! My thoughts were dark; I wanted to die. I didn't know who I was without this job and prestige. I worked as a Bond Broker on Wall Street, it's all I knew and wanted to know. During times of extreme highs, when making hundreds of thousands per year, I recall feelings of enormous fear creep up. Part of me felt unstable. Even when things seemed great, I would feel lost if the money and job went away.

I was high on life on the outside. Unconsciously I felt empty, abandoned, and had no idea who I was. Trust in myself was nonexistent, as was my trust in God. How much of a scattered mess I was on the inside was soon to be revealed.

It started with severe depression, fear, and anxiety. Driving was a task I couldn't bear. I froze up. The thought of driving on the highway or making a left turn paralyzed me. I needed to understand what happened and why I was reacting so severely.

I was about to get some answers. One night, around 3 am, my room black as night, I heard a whisper utter the words, "Psalm 16." Terror ran through my body. In a fear-stricken voice I asked, "Who was that God?" I pulled the covers over me. Fear of the dark, the unknown, and of this cryptic voice that was soft, yet loud enough to wake me out of my slumber, scared the living crap out of me!

My relationship with God was lacking. Incredibly confused by what I sensed were God's words. First, why now? I have never felt protected or loved by God. I deemed myself abandoned by God. Second, why did he want me to read a bible scripture?

Fearful and mostly curious, I ventured on a quest for answers! I didn't even think simply to ask God, because I never trusted him or myself. When I needed answers, I always looked externally for validation. Instantly I reached out to my aunt, seeking support, wisdom, and validation of my intuition.

My aunt, whom I respect and consider like a shaman, is a mystical being full of knowledge. Her essence is pure magic, love, and kindness. I knew she was the right person to contact. I told her what happened. How confused and scared I felt. In her most loving, calm, and peaceful voice, she put me at ease. I listened intently; she told me to seek within and journal my feelings daily. "Read Psalm 16," she said, as the voice instructed me to do so. "Yes, but I did not understand its relevancy to my life, I just did not get the message, Tia," I said to her. She said I have begun my spiritual transformational journey. "Read it again, and ask God questions," she said. Heeding her advice, I wrote all of my emotions and happenings for the day and every day since!

Once I began this inner quest, spiritual phenomena happened on a psychic level. Colors and spherical flashes of free-floating white lights that looked like white globes emerged in front of my eyes. I call these orbs, from the spirit world. The first color I saw was a blue rectangle that flashed near the top of my bedroom closet. It was quite astonishing to witness, something not of this dimension. What was even more shocking was how I felt immediately after seeing this; nauseous. This was the first of many psychic happenings to come.

The most significant part of my spiritual transformational journey is the importance of staying in a constant state of awareness (consciousness.) This is an awareness of my thoughts and triggers, and what is behind them. What causes me to behave or react in a certain way, what causes the self-sabotage? What causes my negative patterns? What causes me to have anxiety and live in fear every day? It took me years to figure this out. I am still making astonishing discoveries about myself and our world every day. The more cognizant I become with my true being, is why they call it a spiritual awakening. I am waking up to the real me more every day. The more I learn about myself and how my energy operates (thoughts create energy and vibration) the more vigilant I become of my surroundings. Learning I am an Empath, and that I can feel the energy of others and of our planet; this becomes a catalyst to my true awakening. I find this out many years later.

The trauma I endured as a child caused the worries, negative thoughts, depression, anxiety, fear and triggers I experienced the greater part of my life. Abused sexually at the early ages of 4 and 11 by two family members, I grew up in a violent household. My father was in jail more than he was ever home. When he was home, fights would erupt between my parents because of his alcohol and drug use, and philandering ways. These events literally split my soul into fragments; so

2020 Shocked Me Out of My Sleep

much so, that at the tender age of 12, I attempted to commit suicide. This day is still vivid in my consciousness; I remember it as though it happened yesterday.

Growing up in a household of fear with an alcoholic and violent dad, I could not trust my environment or him. Terrified of him, I also loved him immensely. Clearly, I could not get a handle of my own thoughts and emotions, and the lack of trust in myself grew. This also explains why I felt so unstable in my life, even when things were great, "waiting for the shoe to drop," as they say. Why money and my job gave me the security I lacked in myself. Most recently, I realized the unhealed wounds with my father caused me to become ungrounded and destabilized.

The deep compounded trauma from my previous molestations and some adult betrayal I experienced during those days wreaked havoc on my pure and gentle heart. I adopted the beliefs "I am not worthy, and I am not enough." If I could not trust the people closest to me, let alone myself, who could I trust? Where was God all these years? I certainly couldn't trust him! These are abandonment and betrayal wounds on steroids!

Let's talk about that scripture God told me to read, Psalm 16. It becomes very pertinent to my story; I just didn't know it then. I re-read this Psalm for months every day, and it had no meaning to me. As time passed, I put the Bible away and did not look at it for several years. Until recently, while writing this story, the verses in this Psalm finally came to life; and I received God's message and all of its glory.

Came to life is an understatement, Psalm 16 was God's message to me to trust in him!!! Psalm 16:1 states, *"Preserve me, O God: for in thee do I put my trust."* How did I not get that until recently? If I had been aware of how trauma and the inner battle within myself affected me, I would have realized earlier on this Psalm was try-ing to calm my anxieties and fears. There were many more messages for me in those 11 verses.

God was telling me he is the one true God, and if I sought another God, I would suffer. That is exactly what I did. I never trusted my inner voice or God and paid the conse-quences several times throughout my life.

There is also a verse that infers God calls us the righ-teous, thus sees us as clean. Another epiphany for me, as I have always felt shame about my past traumatic events and transgressions. With every verse I re-read with total comprehension, I cried with joy. God literally told me he will be my teacher, and will "instruct me in the night seasons," just as he did that first dark night at 3 am and has continued to do so since.

God's message through this Psalm, reassured me of all the love, support, abundance, and protection I would ever need. God has always been with me. He will keep me safe and joyful for eternity if I keep him present in my heart. Did God really abandon me, or was it I who abandoned him? I would soon find out! (Psalm 16:1-11 King James Version)

These epiphanies and revelations did not come easy. The trauma led to depression and anxiety. The depression eventually helped me understand all the shame and self-imposed limiting beliefs I took on about myself were buried inside. I like to take the word depressed and break it down to mean pressed down emotions or old energy stuck in my body. This old energy in my body is cellular trauma. As the trauma rose to the surface, it manifested itself as anxiety and panic attacks. I am not a medical professional, but I have a theory this happened so I could release what no longer serves me, creating space for God's light, and my true divinity within can live with ease and grace.

I lived with this anxiety for over 20 years. Stuck playing the victim, stuck in my past, reliving all the horrors;

instead of empowering myself, using my past as fuel to propel me into a life I deserved and worthy of. It took time to acknowledge how dissociated and disconnected I was to myself and to God. It has been a long road to empowerment and worthiness.

The desperation I felt to experience a life without mental and spiritual handcuffs was something I salivated for. My mind and body were in prison all my life. Determined to get to the other side, free myself of anxiety and depression, and come off my anti-anxiety medication. I've heard the saying, "It's not the destination, but the journey," but I was dead set on a destination. This destination was to freedom and get closer to my true divine self.

On this sinuous path towards my destination, things started getting really hairy during my awakening process. My desperation for freedom led me to do an inner child meditation. I found one while doing an online search. Only six minutes, I thought, no problem. It took me an hour because the floodgates opened. During this time, a golden ray of light flashed twice before my eyes. This ray of light resembled the gold light surrounding Yeshua Christos/Jesus Christ in the pictures I have seen of him. What was God /Jesus trying to tell me?

Shortly after this, the crying and despair began, I burped and hiccupped incessantly. I felt severely ungrounded and dissociated. As the days passed, things got worse. My body would convulse because of my attempt at coming off the anti-anxiety medication. At night as I tried to fall asleep, a feeling of electricity would shoot up my spine, stopping at my neck; this made my body jump up every night for several weeks. One night my fiancé rushed me to the hospital, because I had trouble breathing due to the successive burping and hiccups. The hospital admitted me for 24 hours. The doctors did not understand what was going on with me. My intuition told me this was an emotional response. It was soon confirmed I was right.

An emotional response to what? Nearly 5 years later, which was how long the burping lasted, I would get my answer. Two of the five years I could barely hold a conversation without belching out those Frat-boy burps. My body would scream at me because I was trying to heal myself without medication. I had a sense my body was saying, "What are you trying to do to me?" I was coming off the medication, alcohol and marijuana simultaneously. I was trembling and became unhinged. It said to me, "You're taking away all of my crutches!" My body no longer had anything to hang onto to numb the pain.

43

God was not the only one I did not trust. I did not trust myself to feel. Trauma caused me to mistrust myself and feel unsafe. The burping was an emotional response to the trauma and fragmentation triggered during the inner child meditation. Later I found out the burping's true intention.

Eventually, I came off the medication after 2 months of hellish sleepless nights. I went the holistic route in healing myself, energy healers, chiropractors, etc. One year later, I found out I was pregnant and gave birth to a beautiful baby girl. After my daughter's birth, my mission and purpose slowly came to life.

The spectacular news kept coming. My anxiety kept decreasing, the more I healed and released the cellular trauma, the burping finally stopped after 5 long years! Talk about freedom, I was ecstatic!

Remember the burping's true intention? It was bringing me back home to myself and to God. I believe the burping was my inner child soul fragments integrating back into my heart, body, and soul! It wasn't about getting out; it was about getting back into my body. When I was dissociated and my soul fragmented, I literally had pieces of myself floating in the ether. I did my first inner child meditation without supervision or support; it unlocked the portal where my soul fragments where located. My physical body manifested this action by burping. The burping was trying to bring all those parts of myself back by making space for my soul fragments and grounding them back into my body.

Not only did the burping bring me home into my body, it has also brought me back home to God! Since it stopped, I got a real kick in the ass realizing I held resentment towards God! Of course, I did. How could I not see it? The lack of awareness for so many years blinded me to this realization.

I sat down and wrote a resentment letter to God. I spoke to him as I wrote and admonished him for all I endured in my childhood and young adulthood. The whys, blame, and shame were flying off the pages. The more I wrote and let it out of my system, the more clarity I attained. Suddenly, the words slapped me in the face. I realized it was I who never listened to God, and I felt immense shame. God never abandoned me. It was I who abandoned God. Once I understood this, I fell to my knees in despair.

For nearly an hour, I screamed and cried in agony. I wanted forgiveness! I heard God say, "There is nothing to forgive my child." His mercy, love and compassion humbled me. This moment transformed me; a profound feeling of peace washed through me.

I am learning to trust myself and trust God! Life did not happen to me; it happened FOR me! That is empowerment. All my traumas and struggles strengthened me. In fact, they became my biggest gifts! Could it be my very traumatic upbringing has led me to my mission and purpose? Yes!

The scars heal, though they never leave. They remind me of what I am made of. I have forgiven myself and all who have hurt me.

Forgiveness is another important piece on this spiritual transformational journey! I have faced myself and literally looked at myself in the mirror via a technique called Mirrorwork. Looking deep into my eyes, I released any residual shame and hate towards myself. I spoke to my light, my shadow, my divine masculine and divine feminine, asked for forgiveness, and said I love you, to all of me! It was one of the most powerful and magical experiences of my life. It has shined a light onto my mission and purpose!

I have learned and unlearned during my spiritual journey. There were so many aspects of myself and aspects of the world I was avoiding seeing. They say, "How you do one thing is how you do everything!" This is so true. At the beginning, I mentioned being afraid of the dark. Well, guess what? I was afraid of the darkness within me, scared of facing all the hidden parts of myself and in this world.

Now I look at the year 2020 and realize it's literally in my face. Everything I was denying, all the dark, was coming right in front of me. I learned about the biggest currency on this planet and felt sick to my stomach. It horrified me. Human Sex Trafficking. It brings up the helplessness I felt when I too was sexually abused. It is beyond evil.

Human Sex Trafficking has become part of my mission and purpose. Though it has caused me to feel passionate about helping the children, I am petrified about getting involved in such an evil and corrupt environment. When I think of my daughter and the quality of life I want to create for her, all my fears go away.

It's atrocious to realize there are many powerful and wealthy people involved that many of us have looked up to. Many words come to my mind: I feel gaslighted, manipulated, betrayed, traumatized, abused, and enslaved! I am on a mission to awaken humanity. I am doing it for my daughter and her future, for all of our children's futures, for the restoration of a true civilization, and the creation of living Heaven on Earth!

The sexual abuse I endured as a child is why I connect and relate to sexually abused and human sex trafficked victims. For this reason, I became a Coach, and I am back in school to become a Trauma Therapist. I will be a beacon for all children and humanity's healing and their journey home to God and their true selves.

One day, not too long ago, God gave me another message, "Change is coming!" Once again, terror came over my body, and my anxiety got triggered again (I thought I was anxiety free at this point.) There was no explanation for it. My grandfather had just died, and that was an enormous change in my life, but I knew that wasn't it.

I took charge of my healing, going even deeper to work with my inner child, and grounding my body again, so I could heal this residual anxiety and trauma.

As I am knee deep into my healing, a world crisis, the COVID-19 pandemic, showing signs things will never be the same. The amount of fear I felt was debilitating. I went into survival mode and committed to getting healthy, physically, and spiritually. I could not help feeling shaken by what was happening on our planet. "Change is coming," Now this message makes sense; this is what my body was sensing.

What I came to understand was my body was acting as a B.S detector. My body was feeling everything that was going on. I knew deep down this COVID-19 horror was more than we were being told. I never believed this virus wasn't real; I think it's very real. But I knew something was up. I talked to my sister and listened intently. For the first time, I allowed the information into my brain, and I finally understood cognitive dissonance. My belief system was not letting this information in because it challenged everything I ever knew or taught. Cognitive dissonance is real!

My quest was to understand what was happening to our world during the pandemic. I was on a search for truth. I went to the only source that I could count on telling me the truth, myself and God. I begged God to show me the truth. God delivered! Later that evening, I had the most terrifying and traumatizing nightmare:

I dreamt I was with 2 friends of mine in my spiritual community. They told me something about coherence and tried to explain it to me. All I remember was the word coherence. They said it with 2 words, and

I missed it in the dream. Now, after processing the dream, I believe she was referring to cognitive dissonance. These two women in my dream represented Truth and how it would set me Free!

In the next part of the dream, right after speaking to my friends, 2 human males with hockey masks (one white and one green) were in my room. The one with the white hockey mask walked over to the green mask and stood behind him. The green hockey mask climbed onto my bed and hovered over my daughter and me. He was trying to grab my daughter.

He looked me dead in my face, and I had a second of trying to fight him off; I could not move (almost like sleep paralysis.) In that moment, I was lucid enough in the dream to force myself awake by roaring like a lion. I continued to roar in my waking state and came out of the dream angry, wanting to fight.

When I woke up, I was throwing punches into the air and kept saying, "I do not consent! God/Jesus protect my space." I kept hearing, "You are a warrior. I protect you, that is why you could wake yourself up out of the dream."

After speaking with my sister that morning, I realized

this dream was some brutal truth given to me by God, to wake me up to the evil, dark, and heinous crimes in the world. I have been asking God and Jesus for truth the last few weeks, and here it was!

2020 is the Great Awakening of our consciousness! I now go past the illusions, seek truth, do my research, and not rely on mainstream media for information. My body became the ultimate truth barometer. School never taught me to use my intuition or to listen to God. The external way of learning started with my parents. I sought their advice, their rules for right and wrong, and then to school where I listened to my friends and teachers. Going to a source outside of myself was a learned behavior.

Here is my biggest take away: clearing myself of all trauma, I can be a clear vessel for God to live in. This allows me to feel and filter information through my body. I've come to terms with how beneficial it is for me to remain flexible and unattached in my findings, because so much evolves. The beliefs I held onto have changed. As my consciousness or awareness expands, so do my findings. Truth evolves as my understanding evolves.

It is truly all about awareness. Learning to Unlearn what I have been taught! I choose to make room for fresh ideas and possibilities, allowing for growth and expansion. This new state of being has allowed things to flow and open my mind. Even things I never thought possible, such as the realization of the existence of Human Trafficking and the amount of corruption which exists and how I may be led to raise awareness of this situation.

Awakening to the positive and negative aspects of the world has been a harrowing experience. That being said learning to trust myself and God is the greatest treasure I'll ever find!

"2020 is the
Great Awakening
of our consciousness!"

– Jessica Mariah

*"A new light is coming into
this world. We are on the
borderline of a new experience.*

*The veil between Spirit
and matter is very thin."*

— Ernest Holmes

Deborah Perdue

is the author of several books on her very favorite topic and passion, Gratitude. She also teaches workshops, classes, and facilitates women's retreats on the topics of gratitude, and how to live a life of peace and joy. It is her passion to help others transform their lives, as she has transformed her own. She writes spiritual articles and blogs on gratitude. She has written a Daily Gratitude Reflection to her subscriber email list for over 7 years. It is her intention that her gratitude journals and books will be a blessing to others. The spiritual classes she facilitates encourage others in their transformation to awakening.

In 1994, Deborah received two Bachelor Degrees (Cum Laude) from Sonoma State University, in English (emphasis: creative writing) and Studio Art (emphasis: photography).

Her graphic design business, Illumination Graphics, is a rewarding and prospering day job that she loves.

Residing in the rural Oregon, her home and office are within beautiful forested land, near the famous Rogue River where she, her husband and two dogs visit, and swim in the summer.

Deborah has been a Center for Spiritual Living licensed practitioner for over 14 years.

www.graceofgratitude.com
www.illuminationgraphics.com

Dedication

I dedicate this chapter to all the awakening

light-filled beings I know, who are helping

to bring a new awareness to this world,

into more peace, joy, love and justice.

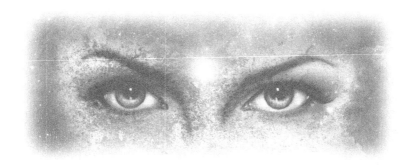

Fits and Starts

*M*y rocker ex-husband and I were traveling home from an all-night drug fest with his band in the Bay Area, CA. It was dawn, around 6a.m. and as we headed north, exhausted and still high on cocaine and alcohol, there were hardly any cars on the northbound side of the road. However, southbound commute traffic was already heading to work. We had sunglasses on, even though the light was still dim. I recall how counterculture I felt. How bizarre it was, like an alternative universe from all the working folks on their way to work.

My spiritual awakening has come and gone in fits and starts. It's been impossible to extinguish and is a constant in my life at this point. I am grateful for every experience in my life, which led me to where I am now. Like most children, I knew much when I was born, that I was inherently connected to God, but forgot as time went on, and the "hard knocks" of life brought me down. I came in with joy and an optimistic attitude, which I have retained to this day. I sometimes feel I have lived two reincarnations in the same life, and the second one, that one I am living at this time, is definitely preferable! I believe that I was always ready to awaken, even in my darkest hours. Similarly, I believe that humanity is ready to awaken, even when times seem especially dim, like they have lately.

There were many crazy times in the 70s and 80s during the 20 years of my life which I spent chain-smoking cigarettes, drinking and smoking pot every single day, and later taking up coke like a fiend. I was often filled with shame. I would wake up most mornings, rack my brain trying to remember what happened the night before, and what I might have done to embarrass myself. Usually, there was something. Amidst a lot of fun, rock music, laughter, incessant talk, staying up all night, this partying lifestyle clearly came with a price; giving me even lower self-esteem than I came in with. During that time, we crashed my car (miraculously, nobody was hurt). Another time, to my horror, I remembered the next day I had forgotten to pick up my sister and her husband at the airport the night before, who came in from their honeymoon in Jamaica. There are a few other humiliating things I did, I won't mention here. Rock bottom took a long time for me.

My mother was a very spiritual woman as she grew older. It was during this time of debauchery in my life, she gently suggested I listen to Lazaris, a wise channel she had discovered. She gave me a tape. One night, even with the mental fog of drugs and alcohol, I listened to it. I heard him loud and clear. He spoke of creating your own reality, and about love and light overpowering darkness. It woke me up from the drug-induced dream I was living.

These are both good examples of the "fits and starts" of my life.

As a very young girl, I recall pondering what God was, being in bed at night, unable to sleep. I vividly imagined Infinity going on and on and on and on until I scared myself and had to stop. I pondered the meaning of life. I now know I was much different from many kids my age. At age eight, I rejected Catholicism because of what I was taught in Catechism. I felt good with the concept God is everywhere. It felt right to me. When we got to the part about everyone being sinners, and how others in the world with different religions would go to hell, even as a young girl, I knew these two things could not be true!

My father was a particularly mean man. He didn't like his three adolescent daughters laughing at the dinner table and would send us to our rooms. He drank too frequently, and any little thing could set him off. One of my sisters was the most spunky and defiant of the three of us, and she particularly could enrage him. He would whip us with his belt when angry. It is a vivid memory of my mother, my other sister, and I huddled together in the bedroom, watching him beat the spunky sister with his belt. Crying and pleading with him to stop, he didn't listen. Even worse than physical abuse was my father's verbal abuse. He dished it out to my mother as well, mocking her and us. When praise was in order, he dealt out criticism. He teased unmercifully too, so I could never be sure what he meant for real. By the time I was out of high school, I was so backwards shy; it was sad. My parents-in-law gave me a book on Self Esteem in my 20s. It was embarrassing to realize they assumed I required that.

Throughout my 66 years, I have forgiven my father at least 20 times using spiritual practices I know of such as Ho'oponopono, an ancient Hawaiian forgiveness technique. (This is an ancient process of finding the truth within each matter or issue in life, resolving it for yourself and with others)

After I am done with the forgiveness process, I believe I am complete, and then anger arises again. It indeed makes me mad that I desire to continue forgiving him. I know from personal experience what Jesus meant about forgiving 70x70 times. Extreme low self-esteem and self-worth I had was because of him. As a result of verbal abuse from my father, I became a people pleaser, learning to be quiet rather than sticking up for myself and speaking my truth, observing how my father reacted so violently to my sister's defiance.

It was around the year 2000 that I realized I was an empath, a highly sensitive being that entered this world to serve. As a young child, I found planet earth to be violent, warlike and shockingly wrong! My desire it to shift myself, the people I meet to a vibration of more light, love, peace and justice. A channel once advised me, that I have had many lifetimes in more Utopian style civilizations and on other planets. Within my core, this rings true.

Between my ultra-sensitivity and my experiences with a cruel father, it is no wonder I made the choice to numb myself out and be oblivious to the "normal" world for over 20 years of my life! Often empaths find ways to desensitize themselves in situations that are extremely hard to process. Some become introverts, shy and distant, others like myself choose a way to escape and numb ourselves, and others get so emotionally engaged and often enraged they are not aware of what are their own feelings are.

My cherished, optimistic, beautiful mother was diagnosed with inoperable lung cancer when she was 56. Oh my God, my sisters and I absolutely adored her. How could we lose her so young?! Even though my sisters had always been closer to her, hanging out with her while I partied, they couldn't handle day-to-day caregiving. It was a good chance for me to get closer to her at the end, and I became her primary caregiver by choice. (By then, I had toned down my addictions.)

After nine months, she was holocaust-victim skinny and dosed with constant morphine. I still remember her big, deep-blue eyes looking at me with love. She was bald and so thin, but her beautiful eyes were still luminous. I remember the "Angels" who came to visit her from the Center for Attitudinal Living. By then, I was in extreme pre-grief, and I saw how centered, loving and peaceful they were. I found out they studied

A Course In Miracles (ACIM), and I knew that would be my next "start" to heal my grief and anguish over losing Mom in my mid-30s. I studied the 365 lessons faithfully, read the dense text and had a profound transformation. ACIM teaches love is the only power, and forgiveness is key to a healed life.

After waking up again, I went to college in my 30s and graduated cum laude with two degrees, boosting my confidence levels a great deal.

As my self-esteem grew and my interests in art, photography and writing deepened, it became apparent that my first husband and I were not a match anymore. We went through another decade of trying to work it out, experimenting in Swinging and Polyamory which sped up our imminent divorce. Another "fit."

During this time, I happened upon a book by Neale Donald Walsch, *Conversations with God.* This woke me up again. I was astounded to find he spoke of God and spirituality in a way which resonated with me deeply. I hadn't felt like I belonged in traditional religions, and he spoke of how each of us is a part of God, like how I resonated with the idea "God is everywhere" when little.

Conversations with God parallels the teachings of the Centers for Spiritual Living (CSL), which I eventually found in 1999. When I was so sad breaking up with my ex-husband, several people from different parts of my life encouraged me to visit a local CSL. This philosophy is akin to Unity and is part of the New Thought movement. Centers for Spiritual Living has been a bridge for me to awaken. Whichever CSL I attend, I find open, warm, accepting people and the philosophy is the acceptance of all paths to God. It fits me perfectly and has never let me down.

Through the CSL classes I have taken, with four years of intensive study, I became a licensed practitioner. The practitioner calling came when I first entered a CSL in 1999. Entering the Center, I knew I was home. With tears of joy in my eyes, I could immediately feel the like-minded people's loving hearts. During the first service I attended, I recall how many practitioners were introduced on stage. I KNEW intuitively I would become one. And I did! The studies entail a lot of inner work, not always pretty or easy, but necessary on my path to become my authentic self, more healed than any other time of my life. We also cast out unwanted, long-held limiting beliefs during the process, creating instead more fruitful, heartfelt, powerful intentions. My calling/agreement made before I was born has begun to be answered.

About the same time that I thankfully found CSL, I met my present husband Peter. He is many years sober, and way more compatible with me. We both had gone through divorces. When he asked me to move to Oregon, I said yes. From the time I was a small girl, being in nature renews my soul. I remember sitting in a blossoming acacia tree, writing poetry and being quiet for hours as a preteen. I am blessed to have lived in the country most of my life, and it soothes my spirit, and helps me to be the awakened person I am. Southern Oregon is abundant with trees, forests and beautiful rivers. Not a day goes by I am not thankful for the beauty, magic and wonder of Mother Nature where I live, in all her diversity and glory. Swimming in rivers, lakes and oceans is second nature to me, and I often forget time when playing in water. True unbridled joy! Being in nature helps me stay awake.

Another super important "start" was discovering the path of gratitude. I started writing in a Gratitude Journal in 2012 and was astounded by how much it positively helped me transform my life. A minister gave out blank journals at Thanksgiving and suggested we write five things we were grateful for 40 days, promising our lives would improve in wonderful ways. Following her instructions, I completed the 40 days, and she was right! It worked. Previously, I had been a whiner and complainer, and I found when I focused on what is right and what I am thankful for, there is simply no room for complaining. I was hooked. Because of this welcome discovery, I got energized to create a Gratitude Journal, filling it with gorgeous watercolors from my soul sister, Tara Thelen, with thoughts from me, and blank pages for the reader to write in their own thankful entries. To this day, I have people tell me how much it helped change their lives, bringing me great joy. Since then, I have authored four other gratitude books. In addition, I have sent out daily gratitude emails for over seven years. I LOVE LOVE LOVE sharing gratitude, and I know it helps awaken people to their better selves, as it did with me.

I'm pleased to say spirituality is a constant in my life now. There is no turning back. I am sober, and have been for over 10 years, and love it so much. It's so much better than muddying up my crystal-clear consciousness! I remember people talking about being high on life, and I thought it was a corny idea, but now here I am.

I know I chose this lifetime to help humanity awaken, and to help the world shift to more peace, love and joy. I didn't remember this until I became more conscious as a teen in the 1960s. I remember talk about the Age of Aquarius coming. I felt intuitively it was true. I attended events to usher in the new age. My friends and I were hippies and living in the Bay Area. It made sense in my heart and soul when the young people of this nation rejected the Vietnam War, and other tenets of the 60s adult society, such as capitalism and greed. I was so proud of my mother who walked the Golden Gate Bridge to protest the war with so many others. For a while, it seemed to me, perhaps naively, that peace and love would prevail. A "fit" in our nation's progress was the assassinations of John F. Kennedy, Martin Luther King Jr., Robert Kennedy, and the Kent State violence by police against the students. These events helped us lose our innocence and collectively we went into grief. I know I did.

As the years passed, it seemed we forgot about the ideals of the sixties. In 2020, it seems impossible to believe we can shift our world, with so much division, hatred and social injustice. However, I do believe light always casts out darkness, and I still have high hopes for us. I see blessings come out of this stay-at-home 2020 year – Mother Nature showing us her rapid healing abilities in air and water quality with less cars on the road; people closer to their families, slowing down their hectic lifestyles and appreciating life more; more workers telecommuting and liking it. It seems less traffic is on our horizon as a changed lifestyle choice. I feel hopeful when I think about the Black Lives Matter movement this year, with young, old and people of all races participating in the marches. I have hope social justice is on the horizon too. This is all healing and transformation. If we are all one, as I believe, then that includes everyone and our precious planet.

You may have heard of the 100th Monkey phenomenon:

The hundredth monkey effect is an observed pheno- menon in which a new behavior or idea is said to spread rapidly by unexplained means from one group to all related groups once a critical number of members of one group exhibit the new behavior or acknowledge the new idea. (from *Wikipedia*)

I firmly believe that we, as humans, are going to reach a tipping point, where so many of us envision a better world, it can't help but happen. It seems faraway but it is coming.

Awakened souls, such as Matt Kahn, talk of we humans becoming multi-dimensional. It is already happening! I was absolutely thrilled to connect with hundreds of thousands of light workers across the world, in a Synchronized Global Meditation, praying for peace and light blanketing our earth when COVID-19 first began. I could tangibly feel the power and transforming energy of all connecting and joining together to usher in The Aquarian Age (still forthcoming!). 2020 has awakened me more, I feel, and I have no doubt I am not alone. It has awakened me in bigger ways than ever before. For instance, I had to let go of my deadlines for the end of COVID-19 (right away!) and embrace acceptance and patience as it dragged on. I got to teach via Zoom, a surprise blessing to have my students come from all parts of the United States, as well as globally. I appreciate social life so much more as we have had to do without it, at this time. Of course, I know we are always connected. Yet hugging and congregating as groups will be very welcome again when the time comes. I miss more human touch and hugs, and attending Sunday services, movies and concerts. I certainly took all this for granted prior to the virus.

I feel my own awakening involves truly remembering we are all connected – inextricably linked – and that includes all plants, animals, other beings and dimensions. If I know this, then I can't do harm to others because I would be hurting myself. If everyone realized this, there would be no more wars or violence. Peace would reign.

Being present in the moment, as Ram Dass wrote and taught us in his classic book, *Be Here Now,* is a way to find more inner peace and more joy. I am sure that sharing love, compassion, gratitude, and kindness are important ways we can shift the world. And I am all in!

Core beliefs which are integral to my spiritual awakening are: God (Spirit, All-That-Is) encompasses everyone and everything; everything is alive, love is the ultimate power, and fear and a sense of separation or evil deeds done are a misunderstanding of the Oneness of all. I believe we are Co-creators with Spirit and since we have free will, nothing is pre-ordained. The future can always change with new decisions made. One thing that never fails to thrill me is thinking of how much is invisible to our senses, but so real. Qualities of love, peace, joy, harmony; other dimensions; angels and helpers; and the mystery and magic which can't be explained by science.

These beliefs have come, sometimes slowly, and have helped me transform from a fairly self-centered person, to a strong, self-actualized woman with lots to give. I do my best to always walk my talk and to lead by example. I do my best to be honest and filled with integrity. When younger, these were challenges. Through my spiritual path, I discovered I would even lie to myself. Getting real is paramount to truly awakening.

Perhaps you are seeking guidance and mentors in your life and with great admiration I share some of the ones that guided my path. These spiritual authors have inspired and helped to awaken me over the past 20 years of the sustained "start" I am experiencing. Some modern-day mystics include Michael Bernard Beckwith, Wayne Dyer, Brené Brown, Mark Nepo, Carolyn Myss, Dalai Lama, Thich Nat Hanh, Louise L. Hay, Yogananda and lately, I have been reading and studying the oh-so-wise sage Michael A. Singer. I also have been influenced by the great pioneers to the New Thought movement including Ernest Holmes, Emma Curtis Hopkins, Raymond Charles Barker, and Myrtle and Charles Fillmore. I am dedicated to my morning meditation time each day, where I study works by other authors, and then get quiet, tune in to Spirit and pray. Unlike the times in my life when addicted to substances, I know this is a very beneficial addiction!

I am grateful for all the fits and starts in my life. Truly, every experience has shaped me into the strong warrior woman I have become. Being addicted to drugs and alcohol gives me more compassion for those who suffer in that way. Having an abusive parent helps me understand other people's emotional pain and insecurities. I was pretty selfish in my younger years, and have learned to give to others, and be kinder. I have become a person to be counted on. I reach out when someone is going through a rough time. This is all part of my personal awakening, which I am incredibly grateful for.

I look forward with all my heart and soul to a momentous shift in humankind's collective awakening consciousness, a brand-new start to a better world.

"We are all equally capable of
spiritual awakening. It may not
seem that way, at times. Some of
us are so caught up in the drama
of our day-to-day existence that
we have lost track of who we
really are. But eventually, all of us
will make the discovery
of our true nature."

— Victor Shamas

"No man is as wise as Mother Earth. she has witnessed every human day, every human struggle, every human pain, and every human joy. For maladies of both body and spirit, the wise ones of old pointed man to the hills. For man too is of the dust and Mother Earth stands ready to nurture and heal her children."

— Lindsay Godfree

$\mathcal{J}$enny Macomber

is a fun-loving, spirited, strong-willed lover of nature and family. Born and raised in Florida, she now resides in in Colorado Springs, CO with her husband, two dogs and a cat. She has adult twin girls. Jenny loves hiking and exploring the beautiful state of Colorado! She has a connection to the diverse wildlife and nature that surrounds her.

Jenny enjoys happy hours with her small, close-knit circle of friends, but is also content sitting alone with a glass of red wine on the patio, appreciating the beauty that surrounds her!

Jenny is a researcher and advocate for wellness and truth. She is currently working on two solo books. A former special needs occupational therapy para-professional, Jenny is blessed to work on her books from home while devoting herself to the needs of her family. She is an Intuitive and Reiki Master, serving as a conduit for Divine energy. She is passionate about the connection between mind/body healing and alternative healing modalities which address the root of illness.

Her spiritual path has led to continued growth and personal healing as she has navigated traumatic life events. She strives to help others by sharing her journey and giving hope, love, validation and empathy. It is Jenny's hope to be a beacon of light for positive change!

"Heal yourself with the light of the sun and the rays of the moon. With the sound of the river and the waterfall. With the swaying of the sea and the fluttering of birds. Heal yourself with mint, neem, and eucalyptus. Sweeten with lavender, rosemary, and chamomile. Hug yourself with the cocoa bean and a hint of cinnamon. Put love in tea instead of sugar and drink it looking at the stars. Heal yourself with the kisses that the wind gives you and the hugs of the rain. Stand strong with your bare feet on the ground and everything that comes from it. Be smarter every day by listening to your intuition, looking at the world with your forehead. Jump, dance, sing, so that you live happier. Heal yourself, with beautiful love, and always remember…you are the medicine."

— Maria Sabina, Mexican healer and poet

Forces of Nature

*F*rightened and simultaneously excited, we drove home on an increasingly windy day as a powerful hurricane made landfall. The birth of the twins had been scheduled, and no one anticipated the storm. Fear, panic, anxiety and helplessness collided with senses of excitement and relief as my girls had been delivered safely. I was terrified for my newborn twin babies as they came home from the safety of the hospital. I knew how to prepare for a hurricane, but as a first-time mother, I didn't know what to do with two tiny lives who relied solely upon me! The wind picked up, became wild, snapping trees and throwing around anything which had not been tied down. The forces of nature were violent enough to knock power out and cause structural damage. With the power lines down and no electricity, we were at the mercy of mother nature raging outside. I was terrified the big oak tree outside our bedroom would come crashing in, destroying the house and injuring us all. My life felt relentlessly out of control and at the mercy of it all. We can only prepare the best we know how. We sit tight, hoping and praying this catastrophe won't destroy our family. We cling tightly to each other because that's all we can do, and alone in a storm. Little did I know, one day this would have greater symbolism than I ever imagined.

I couldn't predict the devastation of one of my daughter's chronic illness any more than the hurricane she arrived home in. Gearing up for this battle or preparing for a new kind of storm was alien to me. A new level of fear, panic and desperation eventually became permanent grief and agony, as there is no cure. My child, who was supposed to be growing up and learning all about life, was debilitated and solely dependent upon me once again. The heartache was so intense it caused physical pain; it was positively unbearable. I could not break from the intensity of this storm. Although my tears were shed in secret, I dug deep, finding strength and courage to fight a battle I wasn't sure I could win. When one member of a family is suffering, the whole family suffers and, so, we have weathered this together.

This mama bear wasn't about to give up. Native American Creek and Cherokee blood runs through my veins, willing me to look deeper for answers. My ancestors believe bears are a symbol of strength and are identified with healing and medicine. Throughout this new storm, I would embody just that. By definition, I resemble a mother bear; fighting even though injured and healing my own emotional wounds. Nothing would stop me from finding answers for my child or being a source of strength for my family. The Earth has always beckoned me since I was young. My Native American ancestry is something I resonate with, the energy echoing to my soul. Sometimes I would imagine what it was like to live so closely connected to the Earth and to abide by her lessons. I didn't realize it then, but I listened to Her guidance and followed the path outlined for me long before I even set foot on this Earth.

Fishing along the sandy bank of a wooded pond is where memories were made as a child. We would catch tiny tadpoles in our cupped hands and climb the low-hanging branches of the giant oak trees! My heart yearns for the simplicity of life then, and a smile finds itself on my face as I reflect upon those days. The pond offered me its friendship and sanctuary as I would seek out solitude to sit with whatever was troubling me at the time or just to figure life out as I got older. Being outside, embraced by the great oaks, welcomed back by the water and the wildlife, fortified me with strength and clarity. I have always been exceptionally sensitive, yet strong willed and acutely aware. Being outside helped me disconnect from the "noise" and listen to my intuition. Traditions from my Native American family had not been taught or passed down. It was their energy I could distinctly feel coursing through every fiber of my being. I couldn't explain how or when it got there, it was something I always knew and felt. In the pond's company is where we connected best. That youthful connection would follow me as I continued to search for peace and strength throughout many storms in my life. I have come to realize human life parallels Mother Nature by showing me how balance leads to harmony and that I cannot control the surrounding forces. My response is my greatest strength by centering myself, connecting to nature, and trusting Divine guidance.

I responded to my child's illness by exhausting traditional Western medicine for the first few years. A friend recommended something some may think of as ridiculous. She recommended we visit a Medical Intuitive Healer. With no answers in sight, there was nothing to lose! Besides, it stirred longings within me to connect with my ancestors through forms of healing and beliefs that defied the modern practices which had seemingly caused more damage than they helped.

Witnessing someone's ability to use themselves as a conduit for Divine healing energy and knowledge was magical and astounding! The Healer seemed to know the root of my daughter's autoimmune disease. After additional testing, everything she saw was confirmed and correlated with the things the pediatrician said when my daughter was a toddler! It was fascinating how a person could have such gifts! Are we all able to connect on some level to our intuition to "know" things which are otherwise unexplainable? I could just envision my ancestors using similar healing techniques! I knew we were guided to her to find answers, healing, and something incredible; the truth of who we are and how to connect to it. My senses were alive and awake, like they never had been before! It was the beginning of awakening my consciousness.

There was a truth out there my soul was anxiously waiting for me to uncover. The Healer's talents acted like a catalyst for my mind, to seek out what my intuition had been guiding me to understand! A longing to identify what I truly believed spiritually and to evolve my own healing abilities propelled me on a mystical journey. Teachers, a multitude of books, as well as my own intuitive guidance, unveiled a whole new world I had felt, but couldn't grasp. Each teacher provided education in something valuable. One taught me how to connect with the 'other side', get messages from spirit, read cards, protect my energy, and listen to my intuition. Another guided me through classes to become a Reiki Master and further helped develop my skills as a Medium. Yet another teacher, blinded by her own ego, taught misguided lessons, which was a lesson itself. They all were. Because what I came back to as truth was in my own heart and in the messages my soul gave me. I must remember to go back to nature, silence the noise, and listen to my intuition. It knows the way.

I am Native American Indian, and in my heart, a belief more simplistic, pure and harmonious is what called to me. Nature administers lessons and comfort. It is in her presence my soul searches for answers and finds clarity. The healer helped to set me on a path which promotes healing through Divine energy and natural supplements, similar to my ancestors' practice. My soul found what I've been searching for, and my consciousness expanded at an incredible rate!

A devastating illness led to a quest discovering a Medical Intuitive Healer, natural healing remedies, and my own capacity to heal energetically. Validation for circumstances in life as part of a Divinely orchestrated tapestry kept making themselves evident. I only had to be open to recognizing them! I realized I had choices on how I would respond to the events occurring around me. Instead of wallowing in self-pity, bitterness and anger, I chose to learn, to become wiser, and stronger. I search for the lessons behind events, just as Mother Nature had shown me at a very young age. Like my daughters, I, too, was born in a hurricane!

The story my mother tells is of rain pouring and the streetlight in front of the hospital blowing erratically, as a hurricane and I announced our arrivals simultaneously. Every single year since, it has rained on my birthday, and on my wedding day it poured! The pastor proclaimed it to be God, sending down his blessings. Native American beliefs see rain as cleansing and nourishing. I see it as both in the literal sense. Water is also symbolic for cleansing things which have become contaminated, such as the air we breathe, but especially our thoughts and beliefs.

Decontaminating a conditioned mind isn't as easy as it sounds! Loud, persuasive commercials convince me I need a new, shiny car or the latest trendy fashions. Social media and electronics seemingly track my every word and thought like a pushy salesman. Religion strikes my heart with the fear of God and eternal damnation for being exactly how my creator designed me; perfect. That's the crux of the whole illusion right there! Let the rain wash away those false, misguided, silly human ideas of perfection! Standing beneath the water in the shower as it cleanses away thoughts and impurities barraging the consciousness every moment is such a beautiful gift! Disconnecting from human programming and searching for sanctuary in the arms of nature is soothing! I want to cleanse my misguided beliefs and nourish myself instead, to find peace and love within. Looking outside of myself for love or validation is self-sabotaging. Appreciating the beauty of the Earth and seeing myself reflected in it and within my heritage is one of the most nurturing places to start. It is where I connect best to my spirit. The harmony within nature's balance, as taught by my ancestors, guides me by example. Combining spiritual beliefs with embracing we are all one connected to the Earth, and sharing its lessons, enables me to learn from nature's forces.

Mother Nature has given me rain as a sign to cleanse and nourish myself. Later in life, nature changed the symbol for me to follow. This time it was fire!

A wildfire was racing down the mountain and into my
neighborhood with 65mph winds fueling its speed! My
next-door neighbor rang our doorbell and pointed to the
wall of fire coming straight for us! It had been burning but
was not expected to come into the city. Mother Nature
had other plans! I had the foresight and intuition to com-
pile our valuables if we had to evacuate. My immediate
response to the sight of the fire was shock and panic! I
thought, "we have to run . . . grab the wine!" We truly did!
As we were frantically loading the car, a bottle of wine fell
out, rolled down the driveway and across the street. In the
meantime, our neighbor is videotaping the fire coming,
knowing our houses most likely would not survive. The
video catches my husband chasing wine across the street
with fire bearing down upon us! We found the video that
night on social media, as we were hopefully searched for
any news about what happened to our houses. The bottle
survived, and we drank it that night. The homes of 346
of our neighbors, including the ones who shot the video,
were not so lucky. Eight years later, PTSD still plagues me:
helicopter sounds, charred remnants of trees, and every
wildfire that erupts, regardless of its location. Coming
back to our house, surrounded by apocalyptic devastation, was horrifying. My neighbor's houses were melted!
Ash, charred metal and foundations, the skeletons of
cars, homes, and belongings were the only evidence left.
There were sticks where trees used to be as far as the eye

could see. Everything was black. In my mind, I still see the fire engines lined up on the roads. The look of horror on the faces of the first responders as we passed each other haunts me. The burned trunks which used to be trees evoke a feeling of tremendous sadness for the loss of my beloved nature. They can't be replaced in this lifetime. Not surprisingly, my house just didn't feel "right" after the fire. A Medium came to my house to cleanse it. She could feel the energies of the loss surrounding the area, and it had resurrected much older energies which used to exist there. I could feel them too, but wasn't experienced enough to be able to identify them. I had also stepped away from my journey of spiritual discovery. Anger about the wildfire and its devastation filled me like a cancer, consuming my thoughts and manifesting within my body. It had left my house standing, but not without substantial damage insurance refused to cover. Feeling abandoned by the Universe, I wanted to punish it by abstaining from practice or belief. I was only harming myself, but poisonous rage blinded my sight.

A session with the Healer restored my "vision". She gave me a rare glimpse of the "other side" from her near-death experience and described sitting in what looked like a classroom. Other souls were there as well. A planning session was taking place for what was going to happen to them during their incarnation.

Some souls were choosing to incarnate for the first time on Earth, others were reincarnating again. Some of them had already taken on the appearance of being disfigured, others were ill, etcetera. The point of her story was to help me understand we plan our path, our traumas, our illnesses and experiences before incarnating. The Healer astounded me with stories of past lives I have lived and how in each reincarnation, I had the opportunity to rectify lessons I failed to learn or expand my consciousness with new lessons. Souls who have agreed to play a continued role in a mutual learning process participate with each other. Some Native Americans believe reincarnation allows the soul to advance as each incarnation provides development. It's funny to me how I had been learning about spiritual concepts that were already a part of my heritage! Being the mother of a very sick child and surviving a wildfire were choices I made. I had also planned to be a student of Mother Nature and learn from her wisdom. Reconnecting to the trees and the animals empowered me to realize my house was spared for one important reason; it wasn't time for us to leave yet. We still had lessons to learn right where we were. Damn, nature sure is smart! And the Universe conspires to make it all happen! There is newfound peace in my heart with the forever changed environment. Because nature brings me healing and peace, I intuitively *know* the pine trees surrounding the house were saved. They stand tall yet blackened. I talk to them and allow myself to feel their energy, which gives me strength and peace. They are my "brave ones" and I have come to identify with them. We have both been scorched and burned, yet we still stand tall in our strength and beauty. The anger surrounding the injustice of the wildfire and its aftermath surfaces occasionally. The trees and the animals, which have eventually returned, have helped me to come back to a place of harmony, just as Mother Nature has always shown me exists. I am grateful, instead, and recognize her lessons.

What was fire supposed to teach me? Looking around from the perspective of my human mind, all I could think or see was devastation. It literally made my heart hurt. As an Empath, I *feel* everything I see. If I step into nature and intuition, I see fire also cleanses in its own way. My Native American roots tell me it paves the way for work that needs to be done while healing. That could not have been a more accurate lesson for me!

I have a lot of work that still needs to be completed.

Every time I start to get lost in my own head, I try to remember I planned my life. My spiritual journey has caused me to view life differently; not as a series of things happening to me, but rather as lessons I've signed up to learn. Two books helped me to understand this concept in a way that gave me hope and understanding. They are *Your Soul's Plan* and *Your Soul's Gift* by Robert Schwartz. The books detail how and why we each plan the lessons we incarnate to learn and the methods by which we plan to learn them. They reinforced exactly what the Healer had told me about one of her near-death experiences! What a tremendous sense of relief! It meant I wasn't responsible as a mother for bringing an illness upon my child! My house really survived a wildfire for reasons I could not imagine! Nature truly collaborated with the Heavens to bring me to where I am! If I just stay centered in that knowledge, then handling life's hurdles might be a bit easier!

My head, heart, and gut like to argue amongst themselves! My head thinks it has always been in charge because it is where all the learned knowledge is kept, and it knows best. My heart feels SO very deeply and completely it understands people and experiences on an entirely different level, so it must be right! My gut is really my intuition, higher self, or soul talking to me (whichever you call it). It is the one who is correct! Sadly, my head and heart don't always trust themselves to understand what my gut is saying. That is the beauty and the curse of being human! I am here to remember I am a Divine soul having a human experience! Like my younger self at the pond, being immersed in nature or somewhere peaceful, takes me away from the "noise" in my head and heart and allows intuition to guide me. I often feel as though I can't escape my thoughts, especially if I've been stuck inside. Many times, I must bundle up to go outside, as walking and getting my energy flowing helps me so much! It puts me back in touch with my spirit. Often, the most majestic of animals will make an appearance! No matter where I go, there is always a place for me to connect.

It is 2020, and I am praying my family survives the global pandemic. Both of my children and many family members are immunocompromised, and the deadly virus, which is running rampant, could prove fatal to them, as it has for so many. This situation resurfaces the feelings of grief and fear which lie dormant within me as the mother of a chronically ill child. Sometimes my sick child loses hope or feels she can't go on in pain every day. I won't lie. When that happens, I falter and find myself losing hope, too. Her twin is practicing in the medical field and is exposed daily to this deadly virus... When her twin told me she was working in a hospital and being exposed to infectious patients; I panicked. I honor the fact I am a human being with human emotions. To ignore or deny those emotions causes additional trauma to my human psyche and emotional stability. I also have a choice, though. I can override the false beliefs of fear and control which conditioned us to follow and tap into the truth of my spiritual being and intuition. I felt it at the pond as a young girl. I feel it in my backyard with my scorched, blackened trees. I see it clearly looking out at the land that breathes the life of my ancestors. I dig deep, yet again, to assure my head and heart that Spirit knows the way.

Awakening to the consciousness of humanity does not just involve humans. It involves this magnificent planet which brings us life and lessons! It involves a power greater than us that we conspired with to experience this "crazy thing called life" (thanks, Prince!). When I am overwhelmed and forget I am a Divine Soul having a human experience, I go outside. I *feel* the trees, the grass, the wind, the clouds, the sky and the stars. I remember I chose to incarnate on this planet, and they agreed to nurture me with their strength, peace, and messages; you are not alone.

Water and fire are two of nature's symbols which have guided me. Water teaches to cleanse and nourish, while fire cleanses and heals. I feel the cleansing nature of fire is more destructive. Perhaps that is why it was given to me later in life. Water washes things away, fire destroys them to ash. They raised my awareness by jolting me into paying attention there were things I could not predict nor control. They taught me nature communicates with us! Finding eyes to see and ears to hear is part of their lesson. I am being propelled to literally destroy misguided beliefs which have prevented me from evolving and to tap into my heritage where I find clarity. My human brain overthinks, overreacts, and lets ego rule my emotions, as it has been taught to do. Writing this story reminded me to go back to my roots, let go, and to see with fresh eyes! Native Americans believe in "spirit helpers" who foresee and aid in healing. My independent studies taught me the same concept for "spirit guides". It is time for me to forge a stronger connection to them and listen as opposed to trying to learn the hard way; by myself! Raising my consciousness means listening to their Divine wisdom. I have come to realize the Healer, books, and teachers brought me full circle to where I began; my ancestry! They are all parallel. In a world where I thought I was defying traditional belief (religion), I came back to the truth of where spirituality began and *that* is what resonates with my soul and what I consider to be absolute.

As a child, I described how I *felt* the energy of my ancestors coursing through every fiber of my being. I feel the same way when I connect to my spirit. I *feel* the love, peace, and guidance of the Universe surrounding and supporting me. Regardless of what is happening in the world, with my children, or in my head and heart, I *know* I planned to be here during this exact moment for a specific purpose and lesson. I *know* I will make a difference because who am I *not* to change the world? I believe all have the power to use our thoughts and actions to make a positive difference. When I connect with Mother Earth, I thank her for all she provides us. Then I fill her and every energy in and upon this Earth with love and healing energy. Raising the consciousness of humanity involves trusting ourselves to hear the messages of our soul. Those messages stem from love and infinite wisdom. We have the power to change the world! We just need to listen . . .

We are here on earth to play a part
To learn God's spiritual laws
When the time has come
We will move on

— Wanda Snyder

$\mathcal{W}$anda Snyder

is a lifelong student of universal principals. She is a Reiki Master, Energy Healer, Sound Healing practitioner and an Ordain Minister. Her work in poetry is a natural experience of her life experiences. She always felt guided and protected. She was guided to Louise Hay's book, *You Can Heal Your Life* and learned how to help herself and others. Learning meditation and connecting to the Spirit world was a great help in writing poetry. She is also an Angel Card reader.

Dedication

To my friends and family thank you for supporting me

through the writer's process. Having Faith, Believing

in God and Praying for guidance is what helped me

through emotional times. I also hope the poems can help

you the reader through your own difficult times. May

God Bless you and may the Angels watch over you and

when you need help call on them. Have Faith!

Messages from My Higher Self

*E*ver since I can remember, I felt guided by a spiritual, inner gut feeling. For some, this knowledge comes naturally, and for others it is learned. However you come by it, you must believe in it and seek it out for it to become strong. All of us have this inner knowledge, the challenge is to learn to listen and trust the messages we receive. I refer to this sense of knowing, this guidance as my Higher Self. It is the place where I receive messages, like my inspiration for my poetry. This is my journey of learning how to be still, listen and pray for guidance. All of my poems are heartfelt, and will always help me call up memories to continue the healing process. They are a source of healing for me and my intention is for them to help and bring comfort to you. May God and His Angels be with you on your journey.

Growing up an extremely sensitive child, I never could quite make sense of my emotions. I imagined everyone was this way. It was not until adulthood that I realized that I am different. I realized that, maybe, my sensitivity is a blessing, a gift.

My spiritual awakening came as a surprise to me. As an adult, married and with children, I decided to go to massage school. I became friends with a woman named Suzanne who seemed very comfortable in her own skin. She introduced me to a healing method called Therapeutic Touch. I had no idea what she was talking about. She asked me to pass my hand down her back without touching her. I did and she emphatically announced "You have it!" "Have what?" I replied, confused. She explained that she could feel the energy of my hand! That I was a natural energy healer.

From there, I took classes in Therapeutic Touch. The weekend workshops were wonderful! The workshops were about *us*, our healing and releasing our own emotional pain. Being a natural healer doesn't mean you are perfect, or that your healing is done. It means that you can help others while still healing yourself.

I enjoyed helping people using therapeutic touch, but I felt drawn to learn more, to do more. Then I discovered Reiki. Reiki is a Japanese form of energy healing that can be hands-on or distance. It is a powerful healing method that is now recognized by many for its use for stress relief and treatment of issues like PTSD.https://www.medicalnewstoday.com/articles/308772]

I eventually became a Reiki Master, so I could share this gift with others by teaching.

I went on to learn several different modalities, such as sound healing, to tap into as many different forms of healing as I can.

With healing as my primary gift, working in hospice was a natural fit for me.

Sitting in a room with someone who is close to passing, certain types of thoughts tend to emerge. You may wonder what is happening within the person; are they seeing or thinking anything? Is it like floating off into to a deep slumber of peace?

Being in this situation as a hospice volunteer inspired me to write poetry.

Walking into a nursing home, I never knew who would be there to see. There always seemed to be someone new. The messages I received with each visit inspired many poems.

Writing poems has brought me healing. Even though I wrote them, when rereading them, different thoughts come to mind. I have been impressed reading books on life after death. Being involved with meditation has also helped me to see and feel things, giving me a better understanding of what happens when we die. Yes, it's sad for those of us who are left behind when a loved one passes. I believe this is because many of us were never taught an understanding of life and death.

Even though they have left their physical bodies, they are still with us. They are still with us in our hearts, our memories. We can still talk to them. The difference is we don't know how to hear them or the messages they may send us. We need to ask for a sign. The sign is usually something you and your loved one would know. That is where you might find peace in your heart and feel their love.

Though my poems might be emotionally upsetting in some ways, hopefully they will also be helpful to you in accepting the death of a loved one.

The poem *"Blue Eyes"* was written about a woman whom I visited, while her husband was there. We started talking and kept her in the conversation, even though she seemed to just gaze into space. I was drawn to the color of her blue eyes. They were a shocking light blue. I wondered what she saw behind her eyes, what she was thinking, where she went and the secret behind those eyes. The eyes being the pathway to the soul, gazing as if she were looking back on her life and making peace with it so she could move on, peace in her heart.

Blue Eye's husband asked if he could read the poem at her funeral. I was honored by his request and attended the funeral. I never thought my poem would be read in public or even be in a book. I saw the way this tribute helped him in his grief and it inspired me.

Blue Eyes

There is a lady with blue eyes
Deep penetrating eyes
Eyes that follow you after you leave her sight
Deep, deep blue eyes
The mystery behind those eyes
I wonder what she sees
She seems to look into your very soul
The depth of those blue eyes
So beautiful you forget
That she will be leaving this earth
She knows when you talk of Angels
She knows they are there
The secret of those deep blue eyes
The beauty that lies behind those eyes
They are the pathways to the soul
Those deep blue eyes

"The Visit"

Usually when visiting the homes, the women were awake. However, this woman, one I had not seen before, appeared to be asleep, so this was a new experience for me. The room had an empty feeling to it. The woman was sleeping, and I didn't want to disturb, wake or startle her. She looked so peaceful lying there. I went over to her and in a soft voice, I told her I came to visit. I told her I was going to hold her hand, to let her know I was there. Her hand was cold and mine was warm. I stayed a while, said a prayer and told her I was leaving. It was the first and only time I saw her.

The Visit

I walk in a room where a woman lies
Not knowing what I'll find
A woman resting her eyes shut
Does she want company?
A stranger calling to say hello
Do I dare to interfere on this tranquility?
This place of peace where spirit goes
I hold her hand to let her know that someone is here
Her hand is cold and mine is so warm
Her eyes open– but she would rather sleep
I wait awhile holding her hand
Prayers and a blessing given
Then I say goodbye till the next time
A friendly visit to say someone cares

Dying

What is it that we fear so?
Dying is body's way of letting go
Of this earthly plane
To a place of peace and love
Where the spirit can soar above
Oh! The fear of letting go
Why do we fear so?
In the silent hour before we go
What do we see or hear?
In place where spirit goes
In this place love ones wait patiently
To take me home
My love ones here tell me: " Go to the light"
The light is getting brighter and brighter
It's time for me to go Silently I go!
To a place where Spirit dwells

Angels mend our patchwork hearts
with threads of love.

–Terri Guillemets

God's Light

Angels are around me

Guiding me to write

Telling me that

Death is to be welcomed

With arms outstretched to greet the light

Fear not the end of this mortal life

The Spirit has no end

The body has only mortal ties to this earth

The Spirit has no end

We are here on earth to play a part

To learn God's spiritual laws

When the time has come

We will move on

To play another part and learn the laws

To play a part until we get it right

Then we become part of Spirit's life

A Spirit's life, stays in God's light

Then the cycle ends

We have finally got it right

We get to stay in God's light forever more

Amen!

Time to leave

My time to leave you is coming to an end
My body is tired
My eyes feel heavy oh so heavy I want to sleep
I doze on and off as if sleeping
I hear people's voices around me
Some voices are familiar to me
Time is drawing near
On the other side I can hear them calling
I see bright light
I see shadows of angels standing near
Telling me I am loved Time is near
The angel of death has come to take me home
Angels surround me
Wrapped in a cloaked of bright light
Oh how beautiful!
I feel love all around me
I tell the angels I'm ready
I feel lighter and I'm floating high above
Oh, how beautiful it is here

Twilight Time

Twilight Time is the time between worlds
The time to make peace with ourselves
A time in a place that is only ours
A place that no one knows about
A place where we learn to let go
A place where we feel the meaning of love
A place where only love exist
A loving place full of light and love
A place where angels greet us
The twilight time- the in between time
The time before letting go of this earthly plane
The twilight time

Sometimes the most productive thing you can
do is rest and let your angels wrap you
in their loving wings. They've got you covered.

– Anna Taylor

Angels

Angels are around us
But we do not see
We talk to them
We ask for help, they give so lovingly
We even sense their being there for us
We believe but we do not see
Angels are around us
Protecting us from harm
Angels are around us
When the time has come for us to leave this earth
Angels are around us in our time of need
Angels tuck us in at night
As they watch over us while we sleep
Angels sends us love but we do not see
Sometimes we are so busy
We forget to look around us
Angels send us messages
But we do not see
Angels never tire
Their love for us so bright
One person is all they need to send them love
To keep their love for us so bright
Angels, Angels everywhere
Someone sees and sends them love
Angel love is so bright
Send the Angels love tonight

When I was just 19 I lost my mother. Losing a parent at any age changes your life. I doubt I've ever dealt with grief that deep. I was young and had not yet discovered my gifts. My mother's death disturbed my faith. As I grow older, I realize that having faith is essential to healing and hearing the call of Spirit.

Death of a Mother

My mother died today
I feel numb and afraid
I'm not sure of this feeling inside
What is this feeling inside of me?
Emptiness and numbness prevails
I go through a vail of nothingness day to day
I go about everyday things as if on
autopilot
The good girl, dependable, responsible
Older people talk to me
I really do not hear them
I'm in a place that others do not know
A place of emptiness, void of feeling
My mother died, some part of me died too
The cord that binds us has disappeared
I wasn't ready for this
She was too young to die
She left four children to raise themselves
She won't be around when I marry

Or, to guide me with my children
She died too young
What am I to do without her?
Life goes on and so do I
Grief that no one told me about
What is grief? How do you heal from it?
Do you ever really heal?
Time heals all I'm told but right now I don't care
My mother's gone
All I do is cry and think of her I miss her so

The wings of angels
are hope and faith.

– Omar M Al-aqeel

Dying isn't always about leaving the earth plane. It can also be about what dies inside of us on an emotional level, about how we bury the emotion within our bodies. The emotions stay with us until we can process and release them. Different therapies can help us through this. It is finding the type of therapy or healing you feel is the best for you that can be challenging. Talking about our feelings can be difficult. We are not always taught about feelings and how to express or release them.

An important part of the process of healing is learning how to forgive. This means others and ourselves. Forgiveness is within, sometimes it this may not be face to face with the person. Maybe in time we will have the opportunity to talk to the person, or we can energetically have the discussion in our minds eye to tell them why we are angry, that we had a lesson to learn from them. We then can thank them for teaching us the lesson. We forgive them and ask God to forgive them. Next, we need to forgive ourselves for how we allowed them to affect us and ask for God's forgiveness as well. Take in a deep breath and exhale. Somehow this changes the energy from a negative to a positive. We start to feel better and things start to change between the person and you. Even when that person is yourself.

Angel of Death

Angels are around on this special day
The angel of death gathers around the child
Waiting patiently to take the child to god
The child and the angel eyes do meet
The child smiles and feels the love
The child welcomes the angel with love
The angel wraps the child in a cloak of love
They soar high above
The child looks at the angel with a smile
upon her/ his face
Feeling only love and peace
Knowing she/he is safe
The little one has taken her/his last breath
The stillness in the room says it all
The other angels gather round
Bring love and comfort to the ones left behind
Trying to help them to understand
God's love will comfort them
To believe that the spirit will live on
Their little one is in God's loving arms
Playing and singing with the angels
In God's house of love forever more
Oh! what love that can be!

The poem, "A Little One Went Home Today" is about my niece who passed away before her 3rd birthday. I flew out to California to be with my sister at the end. I can still see my niece as she was the last time I saw her, laying in the bed, tubes attached to her. Her eyes closed as if sleeping. When her time was near. My sister sat in the chair holding her and wanted to be alone. Everyone deals with the final moments differently.

I honored her wishes. I went down to the cafeteria to see my nephew and family for a short time. When I left, I passed by the Chapel, backed up and went into pray. My niece passed away during that time of prayer.

Around November, the Christmas ornaments were out. I found a Christmas ball with an Angel holding a little girl. The angel and little girl were holding a book and had such beautiful smiles on the faces. I bought two; one for my sister and another for myself. I felt as though my niece was telling me "I'm happy".

As I write this, the tears still come. I miss her, but I know the Angels and loved ones who have passed are there for comfort. Angels wrap their wings around your little ones as they take them home. Our little ones aren't alone on their final journey. They will always be with you because they are in your heart. You can talk to them and if you ask for a sign, they will let you know they hear you.

A Little One Went Home Today

A little one went home today
The Angels came and took her/him a way
To the arms of love This little one went
A smile upon her/his face
Love is in the room
Silences all around
A little one went home today
Her parents cry and wonder why
A little one smiles as the Angels gather around
Welcoming this little one
Angel Love is all around
Now there's another Angel up above
Sending Love to the ones she/he loves
Angel Love

I have a feeling there is one more star up in the sky tonight. Even though it is far away, I see it twinkle - as if to say I'm not alone, I'm watching over you. The star is bright as it twinkles in the dark sky. It is as if it is saying, "Talk to me. I will listen to your hopes, your dreams and stories. Look up and see me twinkle in the night sky. Know you are never alone. For even though I am gone, my love and memories are always with you. I am watching over you, so do not fear. For God's love is always there for you."

My Daughter

My daughter's grown
A wonderful woman she has become
I look at her in wonder
Remembering when I was her age
The world was full of wonder
Mountains to climb
Life to live
Oh! How beautiful she is!
Her beauty is on the inside and the outside
Oh! How God has blessed me
God is watching over her
I gave her to God when she was a baby in my arms
I asked Him to watch over her
I asked Him to be with her always
His word, He did keep
He is still with her
Oh! How God has blessed her and me
Thank you God! for all you have done
And for all that is still to be done
Till the day we are in your loving care.
Amen

I was guided to write this poem in March of 2003. There was a lot of unrest in our world. Many of the men in my family have served in the wars. In World War II, my uncle died in France, at the age of 19. I can't imagine the pain my grandparents and family felt. The pain of losing a family member, and not being able to see or talk to them, must have been very difficult for all who lost someone. And very difficult for those who returned with the horror of what they saw. Military service is also very difficult on the families left behind, waiting and wondering if you will get the call or a knock on the door. It happened to me. My fiancé was on the USS Forestall when one of three bombs exploded, and 133 men lost their lives. The waiting was hard and wondering if he was ok. I found out late that night he was ok. In 2003, the unrest brought back memories and I was guided to write the poem. For those who have a family member in uniform, know God and his Angels are watching over them. Know prayers are being said for their safe return back home, to you, their love ones.

To Our Solders

To our soldiers who are away from home
Fighting in a faraway land
You fight for freedom,
You follow orders, which you took an oath to do
I ask God and his Angels to watch over you
To keep you out of harm's way
And to bring you home safe to the ones you love
Thank God for men and women like you
You help to keep freedom safe and evil from our
shores
We will never know the sacrifice
Or the struggles that you face in silence
God Bless All of YOU
May the Angels protect you!
Thank you for your sacrifice!

Closing

As I continue to walk through my spiritual journey and reflect on the road I have taken, I realize that the cornerstone of my growth is Faith. Faith in my Higher Self, faith in the angels that support us and faith in God. I was guided to work on healing myself and others using different modalities. Then I was guided to work in hospice, and through that experience I was inspired to write poetry. My hope is that by sharing my journey and my poetry, I have in some way helped you. Faith and prayer can be what gets you through the hard times, I know that is what has supported me. May the angels support you and God bless!

The magnitude of life is overwhelming.
Angels are here to help us take it
peace by peace.

– Terri Guillemets

I AM

*I value my beautiful and pure
"Self." As I become aware of my
great inner light, I allow it to shine
brighter and brighter.*

*I give myself all the respect, love,
and self-esteem that I need without
worrying about what others think.*

*I love and accept myself as I am,
for I am the being that I am.*

Spirit.To.Spirit

Forgive yourself.
The supreme act of forgiveness is
when you can forgive yourself for
all the wounds you've created in
your own life. Forgiveness is an
act of self-love. When you forgive
yourself,
self-acceptance begins and
self-love grows.

— Miguel Ángel Ruiz Macías

Gabriella DeCicco

Registered Nurse, Reiki Practitioner/Master, Intuitive Medium, Empath

Gabriella DeCicco has been an RN for over thirty years in Pennsylvania. Being a bedside nurse has been her greatest accomplishment and passion. Her interest in Holistic Health and wellness inspired her to pursue an Usui Reiki Master Certification. She enjoys teaching and performing this beautiful healing modality on clients and has personally been greatly influenced by its healing benefits.

In her free time, Gabriella enjoys spending time with her wonderful family and friends, reading and laughing with her book club, THE BABES, and delivering spirit messages and oracle card readings to her clients. She feels blessed to be surrounded with a supportive soul tribe and encouraged to seek soul connections on her spiritual journey.

In the future, she would like to continue her spiritual education and zany travel adventures with her dear friend and business partner Jen Cairo. She also hopes to publish a deck of oracle cards in the near future and continue delivering channeled messages of inspiration.

To connect with Gabriella you can visit her fb page Soul Connections with Gabe and Jen. Email-gabriella.decicco444@gmail.com or gdcrn37@aol.com

Dedication

It is with the deepest of gratitude in my heart that I give thanks to my God who has given me the precious lessons and gifts that have enriched my life. I would also like to thank and express love to my family and soul tribe for loving me unconditionally. and supporting me on this healing journey.

We All Have Secrets

*I truly believed the mask I was hiding behind would
protect my family, while it was killing me inside.*

We all have secrets; thoughts, memories or experiences we want to keep hidden. Sometimes
we knowingly keep secrets, and sometimes we repress
them because they may be too difficult to remember
or acknowledge. I never imagined I would remove my
mask at such an auspicious time in life.

In my last year of nursing school, I found myself in a
dilemma. My dream was to become a nurse and bring
great pride to my parents. Instead, I was a disappointment to them and myself.

How could a child, raised in a strict, Italian, Catholic family understand what she was entering the moment she 'told'? I tried to be an obedient daughter; yet the decision they forced me to make would cloak me in self-loathing behaviors for decades. The shame and guilt inflicted by older paradigms, indoctrinations and religious beliefs passed down from my ancestors, society and in the collective conscious decided my fate.

How could I face my mother and break the news? Honestly, I could not even look into her eyes as I spoke. The disappointment in her face said it all, and her rejection of the news pierced my soul and still haunts me today. She turned her back on me, dismissing me because she could not accept her daughter was pregnant outside of matrimony. The feeling of abandonment scarred my heart and mind. There was only one decision to be made to avoid bringing dishonor upon my family. The fear of being disowned was so great, it prevented me from expressing my own needs. The feelings of disgrace and unworthiness made me feel unlovable. As a Catholic, I felt immoral and not deserving of God's love or forgiveness nor a place in heaven because I was about to commit a *mortal sin*. (The Church would excommunicate any woman getting an abortion.) Being pregnant in those days as a single young woman was unacceptable. How would I live with this choice?

Over time, and with much help and contemplation, I forgave my parents for being victims of their own generational and religious beliefs. Their own shadows had reflected onto me back then. They believed they were saving me from a hard life. I have forgiven them, but I could not forgive myself for not standing up to them. I stifled my voice and identity as I slipped into self-doubt and did the opposite of what I was taught all of my life.

After confessing my predicament to my family, everything happened quickly. There were no discussions about alternatives. In fact, there had been no discussion before, during, or after the decision until now. On the day of the procedure, I recall being taken to an unfamiliar city and dropped off at the door of a clinic. The fear of what I was about to do was too much to bear alone; yet I proceeded because it was expected. I had lost all hope of comfort or forgiveness. Turning back was not an option.

Outside, people with signs were protesting the clinic, making me feel like the *worst human* possible. The employees inside had told me not to make eye contact or acknowledge the protesters. I was afraid and wondered if they would hurt me or the others inside. They said I was safe inside, still I felt terrified. Other girls were there, and we briefly met with a counselor to discuss the procedure. Shortly after, everything became robotic, cold, and routine like an assembly line. I remember the nurse saying I was the only one who followed the instructions correctly. How ironic my obedience was being praised! Then I exited from my mind and body to disassociate from what was happening.

When it was over, I walked out alone to the car waiting to take me home and never looked back. There were no words of solace or compassionate touch. The deed done, and life went on for those around me, as if nothing had ever happened. I felt empty and isolated. The numbness went deeper each day, the intense guilt and sadness taking me into a state of denial.

All I could think about was I had committed murder and deserved punishment for the rest of my life. This negative self-talk worsened over time, and I was quite brutal with self-deprecation. For years I blamed myself for being weak and selfish.

I secretly hoped someday I would receive forgiveness. I was taught my God was loving and forgiving. With a heavy heart, I confided in someone I trusted about my grief. The confession was met with harsh criticism and judgment. In that moment, I escaped into a dark, secret place. The shadows of my guilt I decided would have to stay hidden forever. The regrets of my actions were so deep my husband and I had never discussed it, even after all these years. That's how deep we shoved the pain and sorrow about that choice in our lives.

Burying grief became normal. Eventually I went on to graduate, marry, and build a family, as though nothing happened. Suppressing my feelings, I went through the motions of life, never fully embracing my accomplishments and gifts. The mask of joy I had created covered up my sense of remorse about my choices, which destroyed my self-worth. Feeling undeserving, shadows of culpability would envelope me so profoundly, I could never believe I was capable of redemption.

Trying to disown my pain and guilt, I refused to allow myself the ability to express sadness or rage. My persona became one of joy, humor, and service. I became a people pleaser, finding worth in how people would see me. What I portrayed to everyone was the opposite of who I really was; at least that is what I believed.

Self-denial, my inner critic, kept me in the negative cycle of self-doubt, becoming my own worst enemy. Soon, those bundled up hidden feelings became overwhelming. My addictive behaviors with food and alcohol numbed the intense and bottled-up secrets I carried for too many years. I looked outside of myself for any comfort. How could I deserve anything good, let alone love, nurturing or acceptance? My own harsh moral opinions became my enemy, my shadow. I felt completely unfulfilled and disconnected.

Sometimes it feels like there are two completely opposite people inside of me. The gentle, reserved side and the crazy she-devil, who often fight for attention, especially when I'm triggered. Whenever I feel threatened with criticism or judgment, I shut down or lash out. I never made peace with my dualities. Now I understand why acknowledging my shadow was so significant. Ignoring the darker side of my nature kept me from reaching my potential and truly experiencing the many gifts I have been given in my life.

Physical and emotional symptoms of depression manifested over time. I was having severe panic attacks and could not sleep or concentrate. Memories of my failures and disappointments constantly plagued me. The despondency and grief made me feel as if I could not go on with life. In my mind, I had let everyone down, especially my unborn child. My emotional pain was so great I wanted to take my own life. Never have I shared this admittance with anyone. Doing so would only cause my family worry and sorrow. Feeling ashamed of my depression and anxiety prevented me from seeking help. What if my colleagues thought I wasn't competent? Stigmas regarding mental health kept me silent about revealing my own needs.

One night, I succumbed to the heartache and washed down some pills with alcohol. Through God's grace, I would see another day. The thought of causing pain to my precious family filled me with deep remorse. I vowed to seek help and finally acknowledge the work needed to be done to heal my heart and mind. This is a shameful secret I have never shared until now. My family doctor convinced me to see a psychologist who specialized in caregiver stress. One of my worst fears was taking off my mask, allowing my vulnerabilities to emerge. What if I lost control and I could not regain it again? My image of how I wanted others to see me had to change. I had to release the need of being seen a certain way to fit in or base my self-worth on the beliefs or reactions of others.

Fear of being unloved or abandoned because of my past was crippling. With much contemplation and conscious work about my shadows, I am baring my soul now. I have learned in order to reconcile my life I needed to step into my messiness and share my vulnerabilities with a professional or trusted friend. Author Charlie Morley explains in his work, *Lucid Dreaming and Shadow Work*, "that shame perpetuates its power from being unspeakable." Sharing my experiences, I realized, would help release its negative power over me. Giving a voice to my experience would help me in the healing process.

Carl Jung, the famous Swiss psychoanalyst, coined the term, *"Shadow"*, which refers to our deepest wounds and the parts of ourselves we repress. The buzz talk within the spiritual and psychological communities became *Shadow Work*, the process in which one acknowledges parts of themselves viewed as dark or too risky to see or allow us to manifest. Mine was fear of my emotions, judgement, abandonment and past. I could only see the mistakes and burdens I had caused my family. What I was hiding from had been preventing me from what I wanted to achieve in life.

The shadow-self needed to come out and heal. How would I do this? I didn't know where to start. With guidance from trusted professionals and loving healers, I began my shadow work. It is hard to be kept down when you cannot be belittled, shamed or humiliated. Accepting, acknowledging, and owning my shame has given me the power to rise above it, becoming whole.

Being honest with myself has given me the freedom to heal. I used to have nightmares about abandoning my baby. Imagining him in my arms, I would ask for forgiveness for my weakness. I had always wanted to be a mother. God has blessed me with three beautiful children. His grace and mercy were further proof I was forgiven and loved. My experiences have taught me to love and nurture my family unconditionally.

Doing the inner work has helped in my recovery from past trauma, mental health stigmas, and low self-esteem. Common shadow beliefs I have reflected upon included: my feelings were invalid, I was selfish, unlovable, a burden, and had to take care of everyone around me, because I never felt nurtured myself. I often wondered, "Why did I have to be so sensitive; Why couldn't I be normal?" Being empathic is part of my strengths, not a weakness nor flaw.

The goal of my Shadow work was integration, bringing shadow into myself to become complete. The bigger the shadow, the more it impacts your life. The first step was self-acceptance, because shadow is born from non-acceptance and judgment. I am learning to love myself, accept my shadows, and bring them closer. Observation without judgment was another important step. I had to allow myself to feel things, without trying to suppress or change them. Silencing my inner critic in a safe and supportive atmosphere was so important to my emotional healing. I had to learn how to embrace my inner child and my complexities. Jung explains, "There is no light without darkness." How could one become consciously aware if they stayed in the dark? My need for self-understanding was buried beneath years of work, familial obligations, the daily news, and illness. I had become hopeless that things would never get better in my life. Worrying about who I was, kept me from who I wanted to be. Busy with our everyday lives, we deny our own needs of why we think and act in certain ways.

One therapeutic way I accomplished this was through journaling. I dumped all my thoughts and emotions onto the pages in front of me. The act of physically writing was cathartic on so many levels. All of my secrets, shame, and fears released through the ink onto the pages. It gave me a sense of clarity and control about what I was truly experiencing. Self-reflection and mindful meditations were also instrumental in fostering self-compassion and honesty. Near the end of my therapy sessions, I realized I had filled many journals with thoughts which no longer served me. In an act of empowerment for myself, I released all the emotional pain and fear into the flames of a bonfire. Having my husband beside me in that moment signified we were in this together. His support had released me from thoughts of being a burden.

Letting go of all which no longer serves me and all the old thought patterns I have outgrown has allowed me to begin the healing. Being human means embracing our imperfections and living life to the fullest, despite them. I had let shadows dim my light and keep me feeling vulnerable for too long. Through learning how to understand my shadow self, I am discovering a person I feel proud to be, someone who can inspire and help many others feeling the same way.

Abortion is a shadow causing pain and unworthiness for so many women. Women are being forced to confront this shadow, whether they are part of the one in four who has had an abortion by the age of thirty or are someone whose sister, friend, or relative is in that count, it is likely there is some kind of shadow around the topic. If my story can help them, then it is worth the telling.

I have grieved immensely for my past decisions, especially during this time in history, with the political and religious controversies regarding women's rights to choose dividing our country. Commercials exploiting the topic for political purposes makes me cringe. They remind me every day of the choice I made as a frightened young woman.

Men with signs picketing outside of the hospital on my way to work helped me come to terms with my own redemption recently. At first, seeing the men with their signs triggered panic, fear, and shame. I fought back tears of sadness and anger every time I saw those protestors. It was like being forced to live it all over again. Then I realized, it brought me to this place for a reason.

God had guided me to the place where I had lost my self-worth those many years ago, to start my nursing career and help others on their healing journeys. My profession has enabled me to find forgiveness in service to others. It is a source of great pride to me. One which has allowed me to love others and myself unconditionally. How could an unforgiving God allow me to be so successful and gifted if he did not love and forgive me? I was truly sorry for my decision back then and I grieved every day. I still do.

As a healer, I often speak of self-love and caring for ourselves holistically. Why couldn't I apply those same ideals to myself? I find it ironic I could dedicate myself to a profession which exemplifies compassion, selflessness, and trust and believe I deserve the opposite. Human judgments have caused so much distress, but my experiences have allowed me to show compassion and understanding for others. My own experiences have allowed me to be empathetic to countless others dealing with their own secrets.

Feeling hopeful, I am no longer afraid to be myself. I was there for people in various stages of their lives. Witnessing babies being born, comforting the sick and dying gave me a purpose. It is an honor to witness the miracles of humanity in all its amazing forms. I learned to trust and feel spirit at work and in my life. It became instinctual to know what to say and do for others. This is where I would hone my empathic abilities for the greater good and recognize the grace I had been given.

Hiding my shadows kept me from living my truest potential and living genuine happiness. Acknowledging my hidden feelings helped me to become centered. It has illuminated my true self and allowed me to live authentically and compassionately towards others and myself. It was easier to ignore my own needs and desires because I believed my darker side would eventually disappear or get better on their own. Owning my reality has given me the courage to discover how to heal my life.

Most of us go to great lengths to protect our self-image from anything unflattering. It is easier to see another's shadow before acknowledging one's own. I often resented my mother for being so critical and even narcissistic. Perhaps this was how I saw myself for my past decisions. I saw her as selfish, because I was too.

I believe in order to talk the talk; I must walk the walk. As a health care professional and Holistic Healer, I often explain how necessary self care and self-acceptance are in our healing process. Our mind, body, spirit connection is intrinsic to a fulfilling life. This realization has been integral to my Spiritual Awakening. An important realization about myself was I could not stand in my power of being a Psychic, Medium, or Healer if I did not believe I was worthy of such blessings. I doubted my abilities because I denied the belief God would ever grace someone like me with this gift. I had to acknowledge my self-neglecting behavior. How could I show up for others but no idea how to care for myself? I could never stop my self-sabotaging behaviors if I could not embrace what was driving them.

I had to make peace with my belief my God is a loving and nurturing one and I was deserving of forgiveness. I discovered this through practicing loving kindness and forgiveness meditations. I remember watching an interview with Pope Francis on his visit to the United States in 2016. He declared the Catholic Church was allowing *abortion forgiveness* as part of the upcoming year of Mercy. He explained forgiveness does not mean condonement. I broke down and cried as I heard the news. It gave me hope I was forgiven. God is merciful, indeed. The abundance in my life is proof of that.

Forgiving God has allowed me to experience all of this and more. I left that clinic one day feeling like shit and now I walk the halls with my head held high because of the work I have been blessed to do. The love and compassion shown to me by my patients and colleagues has helped illuminate my shadows. I feel God knew exactly what he was doing when he brought me back to the same hospital to redeem myself. He wanted to show me I was forgiven, and worthy of his love and compassion. His gift to me was the ability to help others, and I needed to learn how to care for myself. How could anyone trust me, when I was not being true to myself? I had to be honest about my needs and who I really was. This has been my struggle and I try to work on myself whenever my beliefs waver.

Over time and with much soul reflection, I forgave the girl who made that fateful decision so many years ago. I have embraced and brought her out of the shadows and into the light where she could find self-love and empathy for herself and others. Gratitude for my beautiful family and accomplished career has helped me heal from old wounds. All of us have been hurt, betrayed, or judged harshly in our lives. To work with shadows means we can work to heal our wounds, forgive others, and ourselves. It also means we can stop the cycle of trauma. It has allowed me to release the burden of shame, which has held me back from who I might be in this time.

Bringing healing messages from spirit to humanity has illuminated my heart and soul. God would not grant this gift to me if he had abandoned or did not love me, as I had believed. Doing shadow work and discovering my truths is helping me to unblock my potential as a teacher and a healer. Discovering that love vanquishes fear, I surround myself with my tribe, the people who love and support me unconditionally. Only true, pure love casts out darkness and fear. It has raised my awareness that not all shadows are bad and I must embrace every part of myself, the good, the bad, and the ugly to become whole and own the light inside of myself. Tending to and helping ourselves is essential for our own healing, and so we can be the path for others' healing. We are being called to share the role and responsibility of stepping up and becoming whole, so we can support our fellow man and this planet we call home. As a Reiki Practitioner and Master, my goal is to help others on their holistic healing journey and awaken our collective conscious to the possibility of tending to humanity. Sharing our human experiences helps us to become supportive and understanding with one another.

Many of you may wonder why I have shared my story so late in life. Sharing this story has helped me walk the path of forgiveness. Allowing myself the gift of self-forgiveness has made room in my heart for receiving and giving love. I could not carry the pain of hate in my heart any longer. Forgiveness allows peace to enter our lives. In this space of peace and love, we can shift anything from negative to positive. Writing my story has freed me from many years of self-punishment I now realize I did not deserve. It has allowed me to remove my mask and live authentically. Self-knowledge and the ability to share my experiences have given me strength and confidence.

Some of us are wandering through life with false perceptions about others and ourselves. We let judgments hold us back from whom we were meant to be. It is never too late to forgive or be forgiven. Peace is attainable if we choose it. Forgiveness is not about condoning past transgressions; it is about moving forward in tranquility for our own healing. What makes us human are our imperfections and our vulnerabilities. Acknowledging our shadows and those of our fellow men should allow us to be less judgmental, less fearful, and more accepting. Living in shame and denial kept me a prisoner of my own mind. It took me many years to realize I must offer love to myself before I could accept it from others. Choosing to forgive and be forgiven creates space in our lives to grow and love. Do not allow stigmas, judgments, or fear to stand in the way of your actions. Let a peaceful and loving heart guide you on this life journey. It is time to heal past wounds and move forward courageously, speaking and living our truths fearlessly. Compassion allows us to embrace our humanity and provides the ability to forgive and be forgiven. We are all perfectly imperfect. That is what makes us human. Now is the time to remove our masks and live life openly and honestly. Cast aside the shadows that dim your purpose and receive God's abundant and unconditional love. We are all unique individuals with our own pasts and pain. Courage to confront heartache and pain rather than being swallowed up by them leads us to action and purpose in pursuing a joyful and authentic life.

I release the pain of my past to make room for the joy of my future.

*By continuously adjusting my
eyes towards love, and trusting in
God's infinite wisdom, my reality
became full of possibilities.*

— Christanthi Voukatidis

Chrisanthi Voukatidis

Chrisanthi is a woman born in Sao Paulo, Brazil, to a Brazilian mother and a Greek father who chose to make his way to the possibilities of a new world.

Later, the three of them would embark to the Great Lakes of Michigan where they would embrace their new home and welcome their two new members of the family. As a small child her memories are vivid in travels between continents and cultures.

She began her adult career immersed in a family business. With an apprenticeship in Beverly Hills, California, she developed her craft as a hairdresser. Her sense of fashion and excellent work ethic led her to manage a successful family business, The Hair Landing, in Michigan.

Eventually, her love of the ocean and far away places set her on a seven-year journey as a guest relations manager aboard cruise ships. This journey took her around the globe showing her the wonders of the world and the wonders of humanity. An exciting and demanding life filled with adventure and gratitude.

Ultimately, she decided to plant roots on land, focusing on family and by learning the healing arts. She began to build a new career as a massage therapist, developing her craft in Florida, Hawaii, Thailand, and Italy. This is one of her many stories.

Dedication

For my mother

Rita Rosa Daccache who has shown me

countless times over that love never fails.

Free Falling

*F*ather, do you see me? Do you hear me? Please God, help me, read my heart. I trip over my words and they come out wrong. I could see the eyes of God in the vastness of the ocean and the limitless sky, in awe of its majesty, both soothing and frightening, knowing that a moment of bliss could turn into a moment of despair. The crisp blue waters merged with the warm hues of the sky. My senses overwhelmed by the sweet scent that filled the air, the warm gentle breeze that caressed my flesh, the sounds of the ocean like a lullaby calming my tired mind. Here is where I felt closest to my Creator, part of a beautiful symphony, a romantic melody of violin and piano causing goosebumps and tears to swell up in my eyes.

Tears of sorrow for the death of a life I once knew flowed through me like the waves crashing to the shore. Grief overtook me, feeling like a damp dark cloud blocking the warm rays of the sunshine. My heart was breaking open in tiny pieces, bleeding, leaving me weak and vulnerable. Abandoned, betrayed, and afraid, I felt like a lost child, mourning the dreams for my future, realizing the painful truth of my reality. The past two decades of my life had vanished and those dreams were just that, a dream. Feelings of rage flowed through my veins, leaving my blood poisoned with its bitterness, and yet, I felt pitiful and embarrassed for being such a cliche. Just a woman experiencing a midlife crisis.

The ocean whispered my name, I could hear the voice of God inviting me to submerge my body and soul into the holy water, to be baptized, lifting the darkness away. I answered the call. Diving deeper with each oncoming wave, I'd submerge myself as deep as I could go and come up feeling lighter with each breath that I took. Soothed and carried by the saltwater, as if being embraced in the arms of God. I floated, facing the heavens, feeling the sun's shining rays dry away my tears. Peace overtook me as I became one with the ocean, surrendering fully to this moment of bliss. The past with all its disappointments disappeared, there was only this moment of joyful, sweet, surrender. Slowly, the waves began to intensify, pulling me further away from the shoreline. I became afraid knowing that bliss could quickly turn dangerous and the ocean could take me. It took all the strength of my body and spirit to make my way back to the security of my safe spot on the sand. I lay down breathless and exhausted, thankful for the gifts that had so generously been poured upon me. The clouds, breeze, and waves were dancing in effortless flow. The voice whispered, "Let go, surrender. I'm here".

I stood tall, shook off the sand, and returned to my piece of paradise on the bay. Slowly, reclaiming the shattered pieces of myself, trusting that they would mend together with liquid gold as its glue. This time putting my own needs first, not needing or asking anyone's permission or approval. Strong, confident and independent, that's how I felt most of the time. Other times, I would hide the tears of sadness behind sunglasses, lipstick and a smile. Each morning, me and my little dogs enjoyed morning coffee on the balcony overlooking the bay, feeling the sunshine. Watching the iguanas climbing the palm trees, I felt blessed. Disregarding the much needed renovations of my apartment, focusing on its perfect location, homey comforts, the many momentos reminding me of my travels throughout the globe, but most of all, my sweet chihuahuas giving me the love I so desperately needed. It was a far cry from the spectacular views of the city and ocean, with its marble floors and endless amenities that had been my home for over a decade. A piece of the sky with the ocean surrounding me. But this was mine, it was healing. My walk to work immersed me in gratitude as my steps carried me over a bridge surrounded by the tranquility of the turquoise waters, reaching a cozy hotel on the bay, a tropical oasis, a wellness retreat famous for its spa. It was my sanctuary. I felt grateful for this holistic, relaxed environment, giving thanks for the privilege of touching people's bodies, hearts, and souls, which in turn, soothed my own. At the end of the day, the heated marble, saunas, and deep soaking tub pampered my tired body leaving me feeling like a queen. The perks of my job more than made up for the amenities from my former home that I walked away from. Making strides towards the future and feeling proud of my accomplishment, I slowly began to shed my old skin. Little did I know how much shedding still to come. Then one day, I closed the door to my apartment, and went for the ride of my life, never to return.

In a split second, life as I knew it was over. I was hurled off the face of the earth, flung from a motorcycle, falling forty four feet, sending me crashing to the ground. The earth was now embedded deep within my bones and my former self was now dead. The fall should have killed me, but the breath of God kept my heart beating. Nearly every bone in my body was broken, organs were damaged and parts of my flesh had been burnt off. The goal was to get me to the hospital alive. I arrived bloody and raw, screaming obscenities at the top of my lungs, like a wild animal clawing onto life. My body shattered and held together by ligaments, tendons and skin. People were all around me running and shouting, Can you hear me? Wake up!! You're in the hospital. NO!!!! NO!!!!! I sensed an enormous emergency and tried frantically to escape but couldn't move my body, it was like it didn't belong to me but I was trapped in it. What the hell was happening? I kept going in and out of consciousness, drifting between worlds, being startled by the sounds of my own screams. Nothing made sense, fighting to survive, being whisked down corridors and into a cold, gray, room, filled with bright lights, it felt like an abduction. Confused and afraid, I kept screaming, NO!!!! The doctors went to lift me and put me on a table. I pleaded with them, "let me go, I can move, I'm strong". I heard a voice say " Let her try". I summoned every ounce of strength to run away, yet was unable to lift a finger. Realizing I couldn't move, despair quickly overwhelmed me, and like a rag doll, I went from arms to arms. The dark haired man wearing white, so handsome, with a touch that was gentle and kind, he looked deep into my eyes, "darling, he said, you don't have to be brave, we will take care of you". His tenderness and the gentle sound of his voice soothed my soul, I was exhausted and felt safe in his arms. There was nothing left to do but surrendered my armor.

My eyes opened and I saw what seemed like a war zone. People were screaming and crying, as if being tortured, blaring sirens and bright lights pounded in my head and all around me. Fear was thick in the air, like dangerous dark clouds filled with thunder and lightning, the smell of blood so strong that I could taste it. Suddenly, through the haze, they were walking towards me, it was my sisters and my mother and then I knew that everything would be okay. "Oh, Mary, I'm so glad you're here. What happened? Where are we?" She said, "You were in a motorcycle accident, you're in the ICU." "Oh yeah", I said, "Satan, flicked me off the overpass and tried to kill me but God sent his angels to soften my fall". "Mom, please, touch my face." Like a hurt child, I craved the comfort of her touch. Ellen, "get the dogs, I said, they're running around and getting away from me." She reassured me my babies were safe. "Please girls, help me to the floor, please". In my delusion, I believed that I could stretch my way out of this mess and we could go home. Not realizing that my body was pinned to the table, held together by titanium, abdomen still open, and unable to move anything other than my right arm. The pain was excruciating and there wasn't enough morphine to escape it. Crying in agony one minute while fighting for my sanity, and the next minute, surrendering to the madness. There was a term for it, ICU Delusions and I was swimming in the deep end. Unable to escape or hide, I was pulled into an underworld of shadows, hiding behind masks, piercing me with their soulless eyes, violating my body, and leaving me on display for everyone to see. I. C. U. delusions... I shouted, "I see U and F. U"!!! I will not surrender! Apparently, that was my motto, filled with rage and defiance. I traveled in and out of this realm of chaos, looking at all the shadows that were hiding in the dark. Each surgery led to another. Days turned into weeks which turned into months.

Father do you see me? Do you hear me? Please, God, help me. Carry me in your arms and surround me with your angels. My physical body crumbled in ruins and my emotional body trapped in the current of a tidal wave that's pulling me further away, I'm exhausted. I felt a whisper in my heart, "You don't have to be afraid, I will carry you". I stopped struggling, took a deep breath and began to resurface from the deep end. I felt God's mercy, my body felt light, as if it was floating.

The darkness began to lift and the shadows disappeared in the light. The beating of my heart kept growing stronger and louder, expanding throughout my body and beyond, leading me into a new reality of worlds within worlds. A symphony of vibration, soothing sounds and light that circled around me. The angry ocean became the serene Mediterranean sea, merging with the sky. I felt weightless, floating in the turquoise waters warmed by the golden glow of the sun. The clouds in the sky were telling me a story, showing me how to merge and flow effortlessly. My spirit was strong and peaceful and embraced in love.

Nearly one year later, I received news that I would be going home. I should have been ecstatic, but no, anxiety quickly took hold of me. Tubes and bags were still attached to my body that was still too weak to leave the prison of my bed, naked and stripped of my sense of pride and vanity. A colossal mountain, covered in thorn bushes, was ahead of me. I had the strength and the appearance of an anorexic on the verge of death. Unable to stand, how would I take the impossible steps to climb this colossal mountain? After having spent the past year disconnecting from my body, I knew the time had come to reclaim it by being fully aware of my body, letting go of the narcotics that were numbing me to the physical pain, as well as the emotions buried deep in my mind. I stayed focused on my heart, beginning each day with scriptures, meditating on God's love, constantly bringing my attention and breath back to my heart. As if speaking to a beloved child, being careful not to hurt her, I began speaking to myself with kindness, "I'm sorry, I love you, please forgive me", thank you". A thousand times over I meditated on these words for myself and to the faces that I saw in my mind, sometimes it felt true. Careful not to let the weeds take hold, I guarded my thoughts, viewing them like tiny seeds that would grow to be a mighty tree. I would be in control. But who was I? Certainly not this broken shell that I was confined to, or the thoughts of fear that circled above my head like vultures. Clearly not my emotions, that swung back and forth like a pendulum, one minute optimistic and the next minute sobbing. I am a child of God, made in His image where all things are possible. I am loved, part of a family whose wellness was intertwined with mine. I owed my Creator, my family, and myself to not only survive but to thrive. I told myself this a thousand times over. Love would guide me, the love that is kind, hopes, believes, and endures all things, a father that protects his child from harm, teaching us to stand strong and tall, and of a mother that nurtures, comforts, and never abandons us in our time of need. As if in my mothers' womb, I developed from the cells of my ancestors, from the golden age of Greece to the luscious Brazilian rainforest of the Amazons, from the grace of the heavens to the power of the earth. In this stillness and silence, I was being recreated, expanding in this field of consciousness, becoming part of an infinite realm.

Slowly, I began connecting the broken pieces of my body, sending healing energy throughout my bloodstream, nourishing everything from my bones to my skin. Sorting and sifting through all the broken pieces and creating a beautiful mosaic, knowing that if I could feel pain, I would once again feel joy. Soothing melodies and the beauty of nature filled my home. I imagined exploring the rooms in my home, dancing in my living room with my sweet little dogs and feeling my heart overflow with gratitude for these precious gifts. Love surrounded me, from the generosity and compassion of my family to my sweet pets that filled even the tiniest cracks of my broken heart. My mother brought home sand from the beach, grounding me, building a bridge between my thoughts, feelings and body, allowing me to once again swim in the ocean, hearing the voice of God calling me to immerse myself letting the waves carry me and float in the ocean.

But sure enough the waves of despair would pull me under, fear would grab hold of me and I would question if a life immersed in pain was worth living. I'd look at the tubes and bags attached to my body, my deteriorating flesh that was once voluptuous and strong, now just skin and bones unable to support itself. My hair, once a cascade of curls, had fallen out in chunks, leaving only bald spots behind, and my skin was dull and gray. Too weak to move and too strong to die, I felt like a trapped animal. Shooting pains that felt as if I was being stabbed and shredded took hold, sweat and tears would pour out of me as I felt my body being ripped apart. Silently, I'd scream out to God for help. Please Father, let me fall asleep in death. I was not afraid to die, leaving the prison of my body, in those moments it seemed like the most compassionate thing, a way out of suffering from the feeling of being trapped in a fire and burned alive. But hadn't the breath of God kept me alive? Just breathe and feel the breath of God. Digging deep in my soul, I pushed away the fears, grabbing on to faith and fighting fire with fire, exhaling deep breaths, blowing flames, like a dragon pushing away the surge of pain. I'd send my blood rushing through my veins igniting my nervous system, growing, making new connections and building my muscles. Strengthen me Father, help me to stand firm in this inferno, let the flames refine my body, purify my soul, and cast a golden glow around me. A thousand times over, I would breathe through the pain, envisioning myself expanding in this field of infinite light and vibration.

My fall happened in April of 2018, integrating my body with the earth, embedding it deep in my bones, and merging my soul with the very breath of life. This wasn't a tidal wave, it was a tsunami. The price was high, but the treasures are priceless. Time to heal and allow my broken body to mend. Time to be still and listen to my heart, looking at the shadows buried deep in my emotions, listening to the voice of God, and feeling the grace of His golden light. Awakened to a new reality of deeper connections with the earth, fire, ocean, and beyond. Feeling everything and nothing, experiencing the past, present, and future all in the same moment. Connecting me intimately with my Creator and loved ones, feeling how deeply intertwined we are with one another and how every thought and action done in love infinitely vibrates. Time to reflect and choose how I would continue with my life. Hoping that my experience will ignite a flame for someone who may feel lost in the dark, as so many have shined their light for me. Knowing that seeds grow in the darkest soil nourished by water and light. We are linked together, just as trees share nutrients and connect through their deep roots, fortifying, communicating, and supporting one another, helping all members of the community stand strong, in our family, community, and throughout earth. I have been lifted, feeling immense gratitude by looking into the eyes of those who reached deep for me when I was face down in dirt, beaten and broken. Hoping now to reach and lift another tired soul.

By listening to the words whispered in my soul to let go of my fears and surrender to faith, I have felt the grace and power of God many times over. My heart, once again, broken open, this time expanding beyond the borders of my limiting thoughts and beliefs, gaining freedom and strength in the field of possibilities. My dreams are simple, to walk barefoot on the sand, diving into the ocean, knowing that the most precious gifts are buried deep. And to once again stand tall in my highest heels, swaying to the rhythm of the music, losing myself in the weightless flow of the melody. To feel and taste all the richness of being fully alive and enjoy the delicious banquet of planet Earth. God speaks to me through the beauty of nature, from sunrise and sunset, in the glow of the mesmerizing moon, the majesty of the mountains, and the mystery of the ocean. I feel his touch in the caress of the wind and the delicate raindrops, washing away my tears, and in the rhythm of waves merging ourselves with another human being, falling deep into ecstasy. There are so many gifts to enjoy, and to help one another unwrap them when we have forgotten. By continuously adjusting my eyes towards love, and trusting in God's infinite wisdom, my reality became full of possibilities. The spirit of God purifies and refines my body and soul, showing me the pearls of strength and peace at the bottom of the ocean. God, continue to show me the way and guide my steps. Thank you for hearing my cries and comforting my heart, showing me that in the stillness is an invisible world full of light. Traveling throughout an invisible world of expansion I found meaning in my suffering as it awakened me to the gift of feeling deeply alive in each moment, surrendering and flowing in a field of possibility, like floating effortlessly in the sea, carried in the arms of God.

*"Peace cannot be kept
by force.*

*It cannot only
be achieved
by understanding."*

— Albert Einstein

Truth

Closing thoughts

*W*hat exactly is truth? It's perspective, an opinion, not a fact. You have read perspectives of awakening consciousness, and each author shared their personal journey. Did you believe them?

Now ask yourself, is it true? For each individual, perhaps. What if we ask "is it 100% truth"? That changes everything, doesn't it? Everything can change when we shift perspective. You may see something completely opposite. That is ok.

My mother used to always say to me, "Believe nothing of what you hear and half of what you see". These words ring in my ears for decades and have helped me question truth when I am in doubt, when I fear, when I don't understand something.

Think of this: You climb to the peak of a mountain with 6 other people all landing in the same 3 foot circumference. In a circle, looking outwards, holding hands you are connected yet your eyes each see something different and every person will have a different emotional experience. Perhaps your view is exquisite, beautiful lush greenery and a waterfall; while the person to the right of you only sees flowers and the one to the back sees dry land and a road. Yet each of you climbed the same mountain to the same height, connected by your hands, and yet no two will have the identical perspective.

I encourage and invite you to explore your own inner truth. We can do that best when we aren't attached to other's beliefs, opinions and philosophies and lies we are told. Your soul will guide you to the truth, a spiritual truth that provides great comfort and peace in life.

Gloria Coppola

"I cannot tell you any spiritual truth that deep within you don't know already. All I can do is remind you of what you have forgotten." – Eckart Tolle

Powerful Potential & Purpose Publishing

Website: www.PPP-publishing.com

Gloria@gloriacoppola.com

Made in the USA
Coppell, TX
10 April 2021

53356721R00095